PRESENTED TO:

_____

FROM:

_____

ON:

_____

HEROES
& VILLAINS
OF THE BIBLE

ALL SCRIPTURE IS GIVEN BY GOD AND IS
USEFUL FOR TEACHING AND FOR SHOWING
PEOPLE WHAT IS WRONG IN THEIR LIVES.
IT IS USEFUL FOR CORRECTING FAULTS
AND TEACHING HOW TO LIVE RIGHT.

2 TIMOTHY 3:16

HEROES

&

OF THE BIBLE

Real Stories
Actual Bible Text

From the *International Children's Bible*

Compiled by Tama Fortner

A Division of Thomas Nelson Publishers

NASHVILLE   DALLAS   MEXICO CITY   RIO DE JANEIRO

Library of Congress Cataloging-in-Publication Data

Bible. English. International Children's Bible. Selections. 2011.
    Heroes & Villains of the Bible : real stories, actual bible text / compiled by
Tama Fortner.
       p. cm.
    Includes bibliographical references and index.
    ISBN 978-1-4003-1685-4 (hardcover)
    1. Bible stories—O.T. 2. Heroes in the Bible—Juvenile literature.
3. Villains in the Bible—Juvenile literature. 4. Men in the Bible—
Biography—Juvenile literature. 5. Bible. O.T.—Biography—Juvenile
literature. I. Fortner, Tama, 1969– II. Title. III. Title: Heroes and villains of
the Bible.

BS551.3.B48 2011

220.9'505—dc23

                  2011019014

Printed in China

11 12 13 14 15 RRD 5 4 3 2 1

Mfr: R R Donnelly / Shenzhen, China / September 2011 / PPO#

INTRODUCTION

Heroes and villains. They are the stuff of great stories, great legends, and great movies. They are also the stuff of life. In this book, you will find the real-life heroes and villains of the Bible. But what made one person a hero and another person a villain? *Choices.* By looking at those choices, and by realizing that God's people face those same choices today, great lessons can be learned.

Heroes & Villains of the Bible uses God's Holy Word to empower your child to make right choices. Read this book with your child. Examine the choices of these heroes and villains. Then use the lessons presented with each story to help your child see how those choices—apply to his or her life today.

Being a hero isn't about capes, or special powers, or being faster than a speeding bullet—it's about choosing to follow God. One day at a time, one step at a time, one child at a time.

CONTENTS

CONTENTS

CONTENTS

New Testament

THE
OLD TESTAMENT

God,
the Creator

All good things begin with God, the greatest hero of all. And just as he created the world and every good thing in it, God created you and every good thing in you.

from GENESIS 1:1-2:2

In the beginning God created the sky and the earth. [2]The earth was empty and had no form. Darkness covered the ocean, and God's Spirit was moving over the water.

[3]Then God said, "Let there be light!" And there was

light. ⁴God saw that the light was good. So he divided the light from the darkness. ⁵God named the light "day" and the darkness "night." Evening passed, and morning came. This was the first day.

⁶Then God said, "Let there be something to divide the water in two!" ⁷So God made the air to divide the water in two. Some of the water was above the air, and some of the water was below it. ⁸God named the air "sky." Evening passed, and morning came. This was the second day.

⁹Then God said, "Let the water under the sky be gathered together so the dry land will appear." And it happened. ¹⁰God named the dry land "earth." He named the water that was gathered together "seas." God saw that this was good.

¹¹Then God said, "Let the earth produce plants. Some plants will make grain for seeds. Others will make fruit with seeds in it. Every seed will produce more of its own kind of plant." And it happened. ¹²The earth produced plants. Some plants had grain for seeds. The trees made fruit with seeds in it. Each seed grew its own kind of plant. God saw that all this was good. ¹³Evening passed, and morning came. This was the third day.

¹⁴Then God said, "Let there be lights in the sky to separate day from night. These lights will be used for signs, seasons, days and years. ¹⁵They will be in the sky to give light to the earth." And it happened.

¹⁶So God made the two large lights. He made the brighter light to rule the day. He made the smaller light to rule the night. He also made the stars. ¹⁷God put all these in the sky

to shine on the earth. [18]They are to rule over the day and over the night. He put them there to separate the light from the darkness. God saw that all these things were good. [19]Evening passed, and morning came. This was the fourth day.

[20]Then God said, "Let the water be filled with living things. And let birds fly in the air above the earth."

[21]So God created the large sea animals. He created every living thing that moves in the sea. The sea is filled with these living things. Each one produces more of its own kind. God also made every bird that flies. And each bird produces more of its own kind. God saw that this was good. [22]God blessed them and said, "Have many young ones and grow in number. Fill the water of the seas, and let the birds grow in number on the earth." [23]Evening passed, and morning came. This was the fifth day.

[24]Then God said, "Let the earth be filled with animals. And let each produce more of its own kind. Let there be tame animals and small crawling animals and wild animals. And let each produce more of its kind." And it happened.

[25]So God made the wild animals, the tame animals and all the small crawling animals to produce more of their own kind. God saw that this was good.

[26]Then God said, "Let us make human beings in our image and likeness. And let them rule over the fish in the sea and the birds in the sky. Let them rule over the tame animals, over all the earth and over all the small crawling animals on the earth."

[27]So God created human beings in his image. In the

image of God he created them. He created them male and female. [28]God blessed them and said, "Have many children and grow in number. Fill the earth and be its master. Rule over the fish in the sea and over the birds in the sky. Rule over every living thing that moves on the earth.". . .

[31]God looked at everything he had made, and it was very good. Evening passed, and morning came. This was the sixth day.

2 [1]So the sky, the earth and all that filled them were finished. [2]By the seventh day God finished the work he had been doing. So on the seventh day he rested from all his work.

> *God created the sun, moon, and stars, and he created you. He created your heart and your spirit, and he filled you with special talents.*
>
> *Just as God gave the sun, moon, and stars their own special jobs to do in his creation, he has a job for you to do in his kingdom. Each person's job is a little different, but they all have this one thing—the most important thing of all—in common: love God with all your heart, soul, mind, and strength.*

LOVING GOD . . . IT'S JUST WHAT HEROES DO.

THE SERPENT
TEMPTS EVE.

SATAN, THE LIAR

There has never been a villain more villainous than Satan himself. From the very beginning of Creation, Satan has tempted God's people to do wrong.

from GENESIS 2:8-3:24

Then the Lord God planted a garden in the East, in a place called Eden. He put the man he had formed in that garden. ⁹The Lord God caused every beautiful tree and every tree that was good for food to grow out of the ground. In the middle of the garden, God put the tree that gives life. And he put there the tree that gives the knowledge of good and evil. . . .

[15]The Lord God put the man in the garden of Eden to care for it and work it. [16]The Lord God commanded him, "You may eat the fruit from any tree in the garden. [17]But you must not eat the fruit from the tree which gives the knowledge of good and evil. If you ever eat fruit from that tree, you will die!" . . .

3 [1]Now the snake was the most clever of all the wild animals the Lord God had made. One day the snake spoke to the woman. He said, "Did God really say that you must not eat fruit from any tree in the garden?"

[2]The woman answered the snake, "We may eat fruit from the trees in the garden. [3]But God told us, 'You must not eat fruit from the tree that is in the middle of the garden. You must not even touch it, or you will die.'"

[4]But the snake said to the woman, "You will not die. [5]God knows that if you eat the fruit from that tree, you will learn about good and evil. Then you will be like God!"

[6]The woman saw that the tree was beautiful. She saw that its fruit was good to eat and that it would make her wise. So she took some of its fruit and ate it. She also gave some of the fruit to her husband, and he ate it.

[7]Then, it was as if the man's and the woman's eyes were opened. They realized they were naked. So they sewed fig leaves together and made something to cover themselves.

⁸Then they heard the Lord God walking in the garden. This was during the cool part of the day. And the man and his wife hid from the Lord God among the trees in the garden. ⁹But the Lord God called to the man. The Lord said, "Where are you?"

¹⁰The man answered, "I heard you walking in the garden. I was afraid because I was naked. So I hid."

¹¹God said to the man, "Who told you that you were naked? Did you eat fruit from that tree? I commanded you not to eat from that tree."

¹²The man said, "You gave this woman to me. She gave me fruit from the tree. So I ate it."

¹³Then the Lord God said to the woman, "What have you done?"

She answered, "The snake tricked me. So I ate the fruit."

¹⁴The Lord God said to the snake, "Because you did this, a curse will be put on you. You will be cursed more than any tame animal or wild animal. You will crawl on your stomach, and you will eat dust all the days of your life. ¹⁵I will make you and the woman enemies to each other. Your descendants and her descendants will be enemies. Her child will crush your head. And you will bite his heel."

¹⁶Then God said to the woman, "I will cause you to have much trouble when you are pregnant. And when you give birth to children, you will have great pain. You will greatly desire your husband, but he will rule over you."

¹⁷Then God said to the man, "You listened to what your wife said. And you ate fruit from the tree that I commanded you not to eat from.

"So I will put a curse on the ground. You will have to work very hard for food. In pain you will eat its food all the days of your life. ¹⁸The ground will produce thorns and weeds for you. And you will eat the plants of the field. ¹⁹You will sweat and work hard for your food. Later you will return to the ground. This is because you were taken from the ground. You are dust. And when you die, you will return to the dust."

²⁰The man named his wife Eve. This is because she is the mother of everyone who ever lived.

²¹The Lord God made clothes from animal skins for the man and his wife. And so the Lord dressed them. ²²Then the Lord God said, "Look, the man has become like one of us. He knows good and evil. And now we must keep him from eating some of the fruit from the tree of life. If he does, he will live forever." ²³So the Lord God forced the man out of the garden of Eden. He had to work the ground he was taken from. ²⁴ God forced the man out of the garden. Then God put angels on the east side of the garden. He also put a sword of fire there. It flashed around in every direction. This kept people from getting to the tree of life.

Satan lies. In the book of John, he is even called the "father of lies" (8:44). One of his favorite lies is to trick people into believing that God doesn't really mean what he says. Satan didn't tell Adam and Eve to sin by disobeying God, but he made them wonder if God really meant what he said—and that led to sin.

You probably won't see a serpent drop out of a tree, telling you to ignore God's rules. Satan uses other tools now. Maybe it's a TV show that makes disobeying your parents look fun, or a song that makes bad words seem okay. Remember, Satan lies. So check with God and his Word first. He'll never steer you wrong, because he is the "God of truth" (Psalm 31:5).

HEROES KNOW THAT GOD NEVER LIES.

CAIN AND ABEL OFFER THEIR SACRIFICES TO GOD.

CAIN IS CURSED

Cain was the first son of Adam and Eve. As the oldest, Cain should have been a good example to his younger brother Abel. But instead, Cain chose to be the worst possible kind of example.

from GENESIS 4:1-15

Eve . . . became pregnant and gave birth to Cain. Eve said, "With the Lord's help, I have given birth to a man." [2]After that, Eve gave birth to Cain's brother Abel. Abel took care of sheep. Cain became a farmer.

[3]Later, Cain brought a gift to God. He brought some food from the ground. [4]Abel brought the best parts of his

best sheep. The Lord accepted Abel and his gift. [5]But God did not accept Cain and his gift. Cain became very angry and looked unhappy.

[6]The Lord asked Cain, "Why are you angry? Why do you look so unhappy? [7]If you do good, I will accept you. But if you do not do good, sin is ready to attack you. Sin wants you. But you must rule over it."

[8]Cain said to his brother Abel, "Let's go out into the field." So Cain and Abel went into the field. Then Cain attacked his brother Abel and killed him.

[9]Later, the Lord said to Cain, "Where is your brother Abel?"

Cain answered, "I don't know. Is it my job to take care of my brother?"

[10]Then the Lord said, "What have you done? Your brother's blood is on the ground. That blood is like a voice that tells me what happened. [11]And now you will be cursed in your work with the ground. It is the same ground where your brother's blood fell. Your hands killed him. [12]You will work the ground. But it will not grow good crops for you anymore. You will wander around on the earth."

[13]Then Cain said to the Lord, "This punishment is more than I can stand! [14]Look! You have forced me to stop working the ground. And now I must hide from you. I will wander around on the earth. And anyone who meets me can kill me."

[15]Then the Lord said to Cain, "No! If anyone kills you, I will punish that person seven times more." Then the Lord

put a mark on Cain. It was a warning to anyone who met him not to kill him.

> *Cain was the first son ever born. But instead of being a good example, he was the worst example. Cain let anger take over his heart. And then he chose to do something that could never be undone.*
>
> *If you let anger take over your heart, you could end up doing something that can never be undone too. A hurtful word can never be taken back, and some broken things can never be fixed. It's true that everyone gets angry at times, but when you do, follow God's advice in Ephesians 4:31–32: "Never shout angrily or say things to hurt others. . . . Be kind and loving."*

HEROES KNOW THEY CAN BE
GOOD EXAMPLES . . . EVEN
WHEN THEY ARE ANGRY.

THE ANIMALS
COME TO NOAH,
TWO BY TWO.

Noah Walks with God

> *The earth was now filled with people, but the hearts of those people were filled with evil. Except one man—Noah—whose heart was filled with God.*

from **GENESIS 6:9–9:13**

Noah was a good man. He was the most innocent man of his time. He walked with God. ¹⁰Noah had three sons: Shem, Ham and Japheth.

¹¹People on earth did what God said was evil. Violence

was everywhere. [12]And God saw this evil. All people on the earth did only evil. [13]So God said to Noah, "People have made the earth full of violence. So I will destroy all people from the earth. [14]Build a boat of cypress wood for yourself. Make rooms in it and cover it inside and outside with tar. [15]This is how big I want you to build the boat: 450 feet long, 75 feet wide and 45 feet high. [16]Make an opening around the top of the boat. Make it 18 inches high from the edge of the roof down. Put a door in the side of the boat. Make an upper, middle and lower deck in it. [17]I will bring a flood of water on the earth. I will destroy all living things that live under the sky. This includes everything that has the breath of life. Everything on the earth will die. [18]But I will make an agreement with you. You, your sons, your wife and your sons' wives will all go into the boat. [19]Also, you must bring into the boat two of every living thing, male and female. Keep them alive with you. [20]There will be two of every kind of bird, animal and crawling thing. They will come to you to be kept alive. [21]Also gather some of every kind of food. Store it on the boat as food for you and the animals."

[22]Noah did everything that God commanded him. . . .

7 [6]Noah was 600 years old when the flood came. [7]He and his wife and his sons and their wives went into the

boat. They went in to escape the waters of the flood. [8]The clean animals, the unclean animals, the birds and everything that crawls on the ground [9]came to Noah. They went into the boat in groups of two, male and female. This was just as God had commanded Noah. [10]Seven days later the flood started. . . .

[11]The flood started on the seventeenth day of the second month of that year. That day the underground springs split open. And the clouds in the sky poured out rain. [12]The rain fell on the earth for 40 days and 40 nights. . . .

[17]As the water rose, it lifted the boat off the ground. [18]The water continued to rise, and the boat floated on the water above the earth. [19]The water rose so much that even the highest mountains under the sky were covered by it. [20]The water continued to rise until it was more than 20 feet above the mountains. . . .

[23]So God destroyed from the earth every living thing that was on the land. This was every man, animal, crawling thing and bird of the sky. All that was left was Noah and what was with him in the boat. [24]And the waters continued to cover the earth for 150 days.

8 [1]But God remembered Noah and all the wild animals and tame animals with him in the boat. God made a

wind blow over the earth. And the water went down. [2]The underground springs stopped flowing. And the clouds in the sky stopped pouring down rain. [3-4]The water that covered the earth began to go down. After 150 days the water had gone down so much that the boat touched land again. It came to rest on one of the mountains of Ararat. This was on the seventeenth day of the seventh month. [5]The water continued to go down. By the first day of the tenth month the tops of the mountains could be seen.

[6]Forty days later Noah opened the window he had made in the boat. [7]He sent out a raven. It flew here and there until the water had dried up from the earth. [8]Then Noah sent out a dove. This was to find out if the water had dried up from the ground. [9]The dove could not find a place to land because water still covered the earth. So it came back to the boat. Noah reached out his hand and took the bird. And he brought it back into the boat.

[10]After seven days Noah again sent out the dove from the boat. [11]And that evening it came back to him with a fresh olive leaf in its mouth. Then Noah knew that the ground was almost dry. [12]Seven days later he sent the dove out again. But this time it did not come back. . . .

[15]Then God said to Noah, [16]"You and your wife, your sons and their wives should go out of the boat. [17]Bring every animal out of the boat with you—the birds, animals and everything that crawls on the earth. Let them have many young ones and let them grow in number."

[18]So Noah went out with his sons, his wife and his sons'

wives. ¹⁹Every animal, everything that crawls on the earth and every bird went out of the boat. They left by families. . . .

9 ⁸Then God said to Noah and his sons, ⁹"Now I am making my agreement with you and your people who will live after you. ¹⁰And I also make it with every living thing that is with you. . . . "I will never again destroy all living things by floodwaters. A flood will never again destroy the earth. . . .

¹³"I am putting my rainbow in the clouds. It is the sign of the agreement between me and the earth."

Noah was a hero long before the ark. Long before the animals came, two by two. And long before the rains fell. Noah was a hero because he "walked with God"—every day, every step. And when God asked him to do something, he said, "Yes, Lord."

To be a hero for God, you don't have to build an ark, take down a giant, or defeat an entire army. To be a mighty hero for God, you simply need to say, "Yes, Lord," and walk with him every day.

HEROES WALK WITH GOD.

ABRAHAM AND
SARAH HOLD
ISAAC, THEIR
PROMISED SON.

ABRAHAM BELIEVES

God asked Abraham (whose name was first Abram) to leave his home and travel to a new land. God didn't tell Abraham where he was going; just to believe that he would lead him. And Abraham believed. But when God promised Abraham a son, did he have enough faith to believe in the impossible?

from GENESIS 17:1-21:7

When Abram was 99 years old, the Lord appeared to him. The Lord said, "I am God All-Powerful. Obey me and do what is right. ²I will make an agreement between us. I will make you the ancestor of many people."

³Then Abram bowed facedown on the ground. God said to him, ⁴"I am making my agreement with you: I will make you the father of many nations. ⁵I am changing your name from Abram to Abraham. This is because I am making you a father of many nations. ⁶I will give you many descendants. New nations will be born from you. Kings will come from you. ⁷And I will make an agreement between me and you and all your descendants from now on: I will be your God and the God of all your descendants. ⁸You live in the land of Canaan now as a stranger. But I will give you and your descendants all this land forever. And I will be the God of your descendants." . . .

¹⁵God said to Abraham, "I will change the name of Sarai, your wife. Her new name will be Sarah. ¹⁶I will bless her. I will give her a son, and you will be the father. She will be the mother of many nations. Kings of nations will come from her."

¹⁷Abraham bowed facedown on the ground and laughed. He said to himself, "Can a man have a child when he is 100 years old? Can Sarah give birth to a child when she is 90?" . . .

18 ¹Later, the Lord again appeared to Abraham near the great trees of Mamre. At that time Abraham was sitting at the door of his tent. It was during the hottest

part of the day. [2]He looked up and saw three men standing near him. When Abraham saw them, he ran from his tent to meet them. He bowed facedown on the ground before them. [3]Abraham said, "Sir, if you think well of me, please stay awhile with me, your servant. [4]I will bring some water so all of you can wash your feet. You may rest under the tree. [5]I will get some bread for you, so you can regain your strength. Then you may continue your journey."

The three men said "That is fine. Do as you said."

[6]Abraham hurried to the tent where Sarah was. He said to her, "Hurry, prepare 20 quarts of fine flour. Make it into loaves of bread." [7]Then Abraham ran to his cattle. He took one of his best calves and gave it to a servant. The servant hurried to kill the calf and to prepare it for food. [8]Abraham gave the three men the calf that had been cooked. He also gave them milk curds and milk. While the three men ate, he stood under the tree near them.

[9]The men asked Abraham, "Where is your wife Sarah?"

"There, in the tent," said Abraham.

[10]Then the Lord said, "I will certainly return to you about this time a year from now. At that time your wife Sarah will have a son."

Sarah was listening at the entrance of the tent which was behind him. [11]Abraham and Sarah were very old. Sarah was past the age when women normally have children. [12]So she laughed to herself, "My husband and I are too old to have a baby."

[13]Then the Lord said to Abraham, "Why did Sarah

laugh? Why did she say, 'I am too old to have a baby'? [14]Is anything too hard for the Lord? No! I will return to you at the right time a year from now. And Sarah will have a son."

[15]Sarah was afraid. So she lied and said, "I didn't laugh." But the Lord said, "No. You did laugh."

[16]Then the men got up to leave . . .

21 [1]The Lord cared for Sarah as he had said. He did for her what he had promised. [2]Sarah became pregnant. And she gave birth to a son for Abraham in his old age. Everything happened at the time God had said it would. [3]Abraham named his son Isaac. Sarah gave birth to this son of Abraham. [4]Abraham circumcised Isaac when he was eight days old as God had commanded.

[5]Abraham was 100 years old when his son Isaac was born. [6]And Sarah said, "God has made me laugh. Everyone who hears about this will laugh with me. [7]No one thought that I would be able to have Abraham's child. But I have given Abraham a son while he is old."

God had amazing plans for Abraham—a new land, a new life, a new son. He told Abraham that he would bless him with all these things, but God didn't tell him how or when. Instead, God asked Abraham to simply believe. Abraham did, and to this day he is called a hero of the faith.

God has amazing plans for you too. And just as with Abraham, God won't tell you exactly how things will work out or when. Instead, he asks you to simply believe. Believe that he loves you, that you can trust him, and that his Word is true. Then you will be a hero of the faith, just like Abraham.

HEROES BELIEVE GOD WILL DO JUST WHAT HE SAYS HE WILL.

JOSEPH WEARS HIS COAT OF MANY COLORS.

JOSEPH'S JEALOUS BROTHERS

When Joseph's brothers saw that their father loved Joseph best, they became very jealous of him. And jealousy can make people do terrible things.

from GENESIS 37:2-35

Joseph was a young man, 17 years old. He and his brothers cared for the flocks. His brothers were the sons of Bilhah and Zilpah, his father's wives. Joseph gave his father bad reports about his brothers. ³Joseph was born when his father Israel, also called Jacob, was old.

So Israel loved Joseph more than his other sons. He made Joseph a special robe with long sleeves. ⁴Joseph's brothers saw that their father loved Joseph more than he loved them. So they hated their brother and could not speak to him politely.

⁵One time Joseph had a dream. When he told his brothers about it, they hated him even more. ⁶Joseph said, "Listen to the dream I had. ⁷We were in the field tying bundles of wheat together. My bundle stood up, and your bundles of wheat gathered around mine. Your bundles bowed down to mine."

⁸His brothers said, "Do you really think you will be king over us? Do you truly think you will rule over us?" His brothers hated him even more now. They hated him because of his dreams and what he had said.

⁹Then Joseph had another dream. He told his brothers about it also. He said, "Listen, I had another dream. I saw the sun, moon and 11 stars bowing down to me."

¹⁰Joseph also told his father about this dream. But his father scolded him, saying, "What kind of dream is this? Do you really believe that your mother, your brothers and I will bow down to you?" ¹¹Joseph's brothers were jealous of him. But his father thought about what all these things could mean.

¹²One day Joseph's brothers went to Shechem to herd their father's sheep. ¹³ Jacob said to Joseph, "Go to Shechem. Your brothers are there herding the sheep."

Joseph answered, "I will go."

[14]His father said, "Go and see if your brothers and the sheep are all right. Then come back and tell me." So Joseph's father sent him from the Valley of Hebron.

When Joseph came to Shechem, [15]a man found him wandering in the field. He asked Joseph, "What are you looking for?"

[16]Joseph answered, "I am looking for my brothers. Can you tell me where they are herding the sheep?"

[17]The man said, "They have already gone. I heard them say they were going to Dothan." So Joseph went to look for his brothers and found them in Dothan.

[18]Joseph's brothers saw him coming from far away. Before he reached them, they made a plan to kill him. [19]They said to each other, "Here comes that dreamer. [20]Let's kill him and throw his body into one of the wells. We can tell our father that a wild animal killed him. Then we will see what will become of his dreams."

[21]But Reuben heard their plan and saved Joseph. He said, "Let's not kill him. [22]Don't spill any blood. Throw him into this well here in the desert. But don't hurt him!" Reuben planned to save Joseph later and send him back to his father. [23]So when Joseph came to his brothers, they pulled off his robe with long sleeves. [24]Then they threw him into the well. It was empty. There was no water in it.

[25]While Joseph was in the well, the brothers sat down to eat. When they looked up, they saw a group of Ishmaelites. They were traveling from Gilead to Egypt. Their camels were carrying spices, balm and myrrh.

[26]Then Judah said to his brothers, "What will we gain if we kill our brother and hide his death? [27]Let's sell him to these Ishmaelites. Then we will not be guilty of killing our own brother. After all, he is our brother, our own flesh and blood." And the other brothers agreed. [28]So when the Midianite traders came by, the brothers took Joseph out of the well. They sold him to the Ishmaelites for eight ounces of silver. And the Ishmaelites took him to Egypt.

[29]Reuben was not with his brothers when they sold Joseph to the Ishmaelites. When Reuben came back to the well, Joseph was not there. Reuben tore his clothes to show he was sad. [30]Then he went back to his brothers and said, "The boy is not there! What will I do?" [31]The brothers killed a goat and dipped Joseph's long-sleeved robe in its blood. [32]Then they brought the robe to their father. They said, "We found this robe. Look it over carefully. See if it is your son's robe."

[33]Jacob looked it over and said, "It is my son's robe! Some savage animal has eaten him. My son Joseph has been torn to pieces!" [34]Then Jacob tore his clothes and put on rough cloth to show that he was sad. He continued to be sad about his son for a long time. [35]All of Jacob's sons and daughters tried to comfort him. But he could not be comforted. Jacob said, "I will be sad about my son until the day I die." So Jacob cried for his son Joseph.

Of all his sons, Jacob loved Joseph best and gave him special gifts. That was not fair, and it made Joseph's brothers jealous. That jealousy caused Joseph's brothers to do a terrible thing.

Jealousy happens when someone else has something that you want for yourself. Perhaps your friend got the part in the play that you really wanted. Perhaps your brother got to pick the movie and you didn't. Or maybe your sister got to spend the whole day with Mom doing something fun. Jealousy can slip into your heart before you know it. When it does, what will you do? Will you throw a fit, whine, or pout? Or will you choose to think about the many blessings that you do have and be thankful? God wants you to "always be thankful" (Colossians 3:15).

A TRUE HERO HAS A THANKFUL HEART.

POTIPHAR'S WIFE LIES

Even though Joseph was sold into slavery, he chose to work hard, and God was with Joseph. But when his master's wife tempted him to do wrong, was Joseph able to stand strong?

from **GENESIS 39:1-23**

Now Joseph had been taken down to Egypt. An Egyptian named Potiphar was an officer to the king of Egypt. He was the captain of the palace guard. He bought Joseph from the Ishmaelites who had brought him down there. [2]The Lord was with Joseph, and he became a successful man. He lived in the house of his master, Potiphar the Egyptian.

[3]Potiphar saw that the Lord was with Joseph. He saw that the Lord made Joseph successful in everything he did. [4]So Potiphar was very happy with Joseph. He allowed Joseph to be his personal servant. He put Joseph in charge of the house. Joseph was trusted with everything Potiphar owned. [5]So Joseph was put in charge of the house. He was put in charge of everything Potiphar owned. Then the Lord blessed the people in Potiphar's house because of Joseph. And the Lord blessed everything that belonged to Potiphar, both in the house and in the field. [6]So Potiphar put Joseph in charge of everything he owned. Potiphar was not concerned about anything, except the food he ate.

Now Joseph was well built and handsome. [7]After some time the wife of Joseph's master began to desire Joseph. One day she said to him, "Have sexual relations with me."

[8]But Joseph refused. He said to her, "My master trusts me with everything in his house. He has put me in charge of everything he owns. [9]There is no one in his house greater than I. He has not kept anything from me, except you. And that is because you are his wife. How can I do such an evil thing? It is a sin against God."

[10]The woman talked to Joseph every day, but he refused to have sexual relations with her or even spend time with her.

[11]One day Joseph went into the house to do his work as

usual. He was the only man in the house at that time. [12]His master's wife grabbed his coat. She said to him, "Come and have sexual relations with me." But Joseph left his coat in her hand and ran out of the house.

[13]She saw what Joseph had done. He had left his coat in her hands and had run outside. [14]So she called to the servants in her house. She said, "Look! This Hebrew slave was brought here to shame us. He came in and tried to have sexual relations with me. But I screamed. [15]My scream scared him, and he ran away. But he left his coat with me." [16]She kept his coat until her husband came home. [17]And she told her husband the same story. She said, "This Hebrew slave you brought here came in to shame me! [18]When he came near me, I screamed. He ran away, but he left his coat."

[19]When Joseph's master heard what his wife said Joseph had done, he became very angry. [20]So Potiphar arrested Joseph and put him into prison. This prison was where the king's prisoners were put. And Joseph stayed there in the prison.

[21]But the Lord was with Joseph and showed him kindness. The Lord caused the prison warden to like Joseph. [22]The prison warden chose Joseph to take care of all the prisoners. He was responsible for whatever was done in the prison. [23]The warden paid no attention to anything that was in Joseph's care. This was because the Lord was with Joseph. The Lord made Joseph successful in everything he did.

Potiphar's wife tried to get Joseph to do something that was wrong. First, she tempted him, then she tricked him, and finally—when her wicked plans failed—she lied about it. One wrong thing led to another wrong thing and then another—until Joseph, who was innocent, ended up in jail.

It's so easy for one little wrong thing to lead to another. Forgotten homework can lead to a tiny fib, which can lead to cheating on a test and an even bigger fib!

Even God's heroes make mistakes. But "if you hide your sins, you will not succeed" (Proverbs 28:13). Tell God instead, and he will forgive you.

GOD'S HEROES KNOW THAT YOU CAN'T FIX ONE WRONG WITH ANOTHER WRONG.

Joseph Forgives

The king of Egypt had a dream that no one could explain. So when the king heard that Joseph could explain dreams, he had him brought from prison. With God's help, Joseph told the king that seven years of good crops would be followed by seven years of famine. So the king put Joseph in charge of storing up the grain throughout all of Egypt.

from **GENESIS 41:46–45:11**

Joseph was 30 years old when he began serving the king of Egypt. And he left the king's court and traveled through all the land of Egypt. [47]During the seven good years, the crops in the land grew well. [48]And Joseph gathered all the food which was produced in Egypt during those seven years of good crops. He stored the food in the cities. In every city he stored grain that had been grown in the fields around that city. [49]Joseph stored much grain, as much as the sand of the seashore. He stored so much grain that he could not measure it. . . .

[53]The seven years of good crops came to an end in the land of Egypt. [54]Then the seven years of hunger began, just as Joseph had said. In all the lands people had nothing to eat. But in Egypt there was food. [55]The time of hunger became terrible in all of Egypt. The people cried out to the king for food. He said to all the Egyptians, "Go to Joseph. Do whatever he tells you to do."

[56]The hunger was everywhere in that part of the world. And Joseph opened the storehouses and sold grain to the people of Egypt. This was because the time of hunger became terrible in Egypt. [57]And all the people in that part of the world came to Joseph in Egypt to buy grain. This was because the hunger was terrible everywhere in that part of the world.

42 [1]Jacob learned that there was grain in Egypt. So he said to his sons . . . [2]"Go down there and buy grain for us to eat. Then we will live and not die."

[3]So ten of Joseph's brothers went down to buy grain from Egypt. [4]But Jacob did not send Benjamin, Joseph's brother, with them. Jacob was afraid that something terrible might happen to Benjamin. . . .

[6]Now Joseph was governor over Egypt. He was the

one who sold the grain to people who came to buy it. So Joseph's brothers came to him. They bowed facedown on the ground before him. ⁷When Joseph saw his brothers, he knew who they were. But he acted as if he didn't know them. He asked unkindly, "Where do you come from?"

They answered, "We have come from the land of Canaan to buy food." . . .

¹²Then Joseph said to them, "No! You have come to learn where this nation is weak!"

¹³And they said, "We are 10 of 12 brothers. We are sons of the same father. We live in the land of Canaan. Our youngest brother is there with our father right now. And our other brother is gone."

¹⁴But Joseph said to them, "I can see I was right! You are spies! . . . ¹⁹If you are honest men, let one of your brothers stay here in prison. The rest of you go and carry grain back to feed your hungry families. ²⁰Then bring your youngest brother back here to me. If you do this, I will know you are telling the truth. Then you will not die." The brothers agreed to this. . . .

²⁶So the brothers put the grain on their donkeys and left. ²⁷When they stopped for the night, one of the brothers opened his sack. He was going to get food for his donkey. Then he saw his money in the top of the sack. ²⁸He said

to the other brothers, "The money I paid for the grain has been put back. Here it is in my sack!"

The brothers were very frightened. They said to each other, "What has God done to us?"

²⁹The brothers went to their father Jacob in the land of Canaan. They told him everything that had happened. . . .

³⁵Then the brothers emptied their sacks. And each of them found his money in his sack. When they and their father saw it, they were afraid. . . .

43 ¹Still no food grew in the land of Canaan. ²Jacob's family had eaten all the grain they had brought from Egypt. So Jacob said to them, "Go to Egypt again. Buy a little more grain for us to eat."

³But Judah said to Jacob, "The governor of that country strongly warned us. He said, 'Bring your brother back with you. If you don't, you will not be allowed to see me.' ⁴If you will send Benjamin with us, we will go down and buy food for you. ⁵But if you refuse to send Benjamin, we will not go." . . .

¹¹Jacob said to them, . . .¹² "Take twice as much money with you this time. Take back the money that was returned to you in your sacks last time. Maybe it was a mistake. ¹³And take Benjamin with you. Now leave and go to the man." . . .

¹⁵So the brothers took the gifts. They also took twice as much money as they had taken the first time. And they took Benjamin. They hurried down to Egypt and stood before Joseph.

¹⁶In Egypt Joseph saw Benjamin with them. Joseph said to the servant in charge of his house, "Bring those men into my house. Kill an animal and prepare a meal. Those men will eat with me today at noon." ¹⁷The servant did as Joseph told him. He brought the men to Joseph's house.

¹⁸The brothers were afraid . . .

²⁹Then Joseph saw his brother Benjamin, who had the same mother as he. Joseph asked, "Is this your youngest brother you told me about?" Then Joseph said to Benjamin, "God be good to you, my son!" ³⁰Then Joseph hurried off. He had to hold back the tears when he saw his brother Benjamin. So Joseph went into his room and cried there. ³¹Then he washed his face and came out. He controlled himself and said, "Serve the meal." . . . ³⁴But Benjamin was given five times more food than the others.

44 ¹Then Joseph gave a command to the servant in charge of his house. Joseph said, "Fill the men's sacks with as much grain as they can carry. And put each man's money into his sack with the grain. ²Put my silver cup in the sack of the youngest brother. Also put his money for the grain in that sack." The servant did what Joseph told him.

³At dawn the brothers were sent away with their donkeys. ⁴They were not far from the city when Joseph said

to the servant in charge of his house, "Go after the men. When you catch up with them, say, 'Why have you paid back evil for good? [5]The cup you have stolen is the one my master uses for drinking. And he uses it for explaining dreams. You have done a very wicked thing!'"

[6]So the servant caught up with the brothers. He said to them what Joseph had told him to say.

[7]But the brothers said to the servant, "Why do you say these things? We would not do anything like that! [8]We brought back to you the money we found in our sacks. We brought it back from the land of Canaan. So surely we would not steal silver or gold from your master's house. [9]If you find that silver cup in the sack of one of us, then let him die. And we will be your slaves." . . .

[11]Then every brother quickly lowered his sack to the ground and opened it. [12]The servant searched the sacks, going from the oldest brother to the youngest. He found the cup in Benjamin's sack. [13]The brothers tore their clothes to show they were sad. Then they put their sacks back on the donkeys. And they returned to the city.

[14]When Judah and his brothers went back to Joseph's house, Joseph was still there. The brothers bowed facedown on the ground before him. [15]Joseph said to them, "What have you done? Didn't you know that a man like me can learn things by signs and dreams?"

[16]Judah said, "Sir, what can we say? And how can we show we are not guilty? God has uncovered our guilt. So all of us will be your slaves, not just Benjamin."

[17]But Joseph said, "I will not make you all slaves! Only the man who stole the cup will be my slave. The rest of you may go back safely to your father."

[18]Then Judah went to Joseph and said, "Sir, please let me speak plainly to you. Please don't be angry with me. I know that you are as powerful as the king of Egypt himself. [19]When we were here before, you asked us, 'Do you have a father or a brother?' [20]And we answered you, 'We have an old father. And we have a younger brother. He was born when our father was old. This youngest son's brother is dead. So he is the only one of his mother's children left alive. And our father loves him very much.' [21]Then you said to us, 'Bring that brother to me. I want to see him.' [22]And we said to you, 'That young boy cannot leave his father. If he leaves him, his father would die.' [23]But you said to us, 'You must bring your youngest brother. If you don't, you will not be allowed to see me again.' [24]So we went back to our father and told him what you had said.

[25]"Later, our father said, 'Go again. Buy us a little more food.' [26]We said to our father, 'We cannot go without our youngest brother. Without our youngest brother, we will not be allowed to see the governor.' [27]Then my father said to us, 'You know that my wife Rachel gave me two sons. [28]One son left me. I thought, "Surely he has been torn apart by a wild animal." And I haven't seen him since. [29]Now you want to take this son away from me also. But something terrible might happen to him. Then I would be sad until the day I die.' [30]Now what will happen if we go home to our father without

our youngest brother? He is the most important thing in our father's life. ³¹When our father sees that the young boy is not with us, he will die. And it will be our fault. We will cause the great sorrow that kills our father.

³²"I gave my father a guarantee that the young boy would be safe. I said to my father, 'If I don't bring him back to you, you can blame me all my life.' ³³So now, please allow me to stay here and be your slave. And let the young boy go back home with his brothers. ³⁴I cannot go back to my father if the boy is not with me. I couldn't stand to see my father that sad."

45 ¹Joseph could not control himself in front of his servants any longer. He cried out, "Have everyone leave me." When only the brothers were left with Joseph, he told them who he was. ²Joseph cried so loudly that the Egyptians heard him. And the people in the king's palace heard about it. ³He said to his brothers, "I am Joseph. Is my father still alive?" But the brothers could not answer him, because they were very afraid of him.

⁴So Joseph said to them, "Come close to me." So the brothers came close to him. And he said to them, "I am your brother Joseph. You sold me as a slave to go to Egypt. ⁵Now don't be worried. Don't be angry with yourselves because you sold me here. God sent me here ahead of you to save people's lives. . . . ⁷And it was to keep you alive in an amazing way. ⁸So it was not you who sent me here, but God. God has made me the highest officer of the king of Egypt. I am in charge of his palace. I am the master of all the land of Egypt.

[9]"So leave quickly and go to my father. Tell him, 'Your son Joseph says: God has made me master over all Egypt. Come down to me quickly. [10]Live in the land of Goshen. You will be near me. Also your children, your grandchildren, your flocks and herds and all that you have will be near me. [11]I will care for you during the next five years of hunger. In this way, you and your family and all that you have will not starve.'"

Joseph had very good reasons to be angry at his brothers. He had been taken from his home, sold as a slave, and thrown in prison—and it was their fault! Now that Joseph was a powerful man in Egypt, he could have chosen to punish his brothers, but he chose to forgive them instead.

You may have a good reason to be angry with someone. Perhaps your friend cheated in a game. Perhaps your brother or sister took something without asking. You have to make the same choice Joseph did—punish them with your anger, or forgive them. God hopes that you will choose to forgive, "just as God forgave you in Christ" (Ephesians 4:32).

FORGIVING OTHERS IS
WHAT HEROES DO.

Miriam Watches over Moses

A new and terrible king had come to rule the land of Egypt. But terrible villains call for great heroes—and heroes can come in all shapes and sizes.

from EXODUS 1:8-2:10

Then a new king began to rule Egypt. He did not know who Joseph was. ⁹This king said to his people, "Look! The people of Israel are too many! And they are too strong for us to handle! ¹⁰We must make plans against them. If we don't, the number of their people will grow even more. Then if there is a war, they might join our enemies. Then they could fight us and escape from the country!"

[11]So the Egyptians made life hard for the people of Israel. They put slave masters over the Israelites. The slave masters forced the Israelites to build the cities Pithom and Rameses for the king. These cities were supply centers in which the Egyptians stored things. [12]The Egyptians forced the Israelites to work even harder. But this made the Israelites grow in number and spread more. So the Egyptians became more afraid of them. [13]They forced the Israelites to work even harder. [14]The Egyptians made life hard for the Israelites. They forced the Israelites to work very hard making bricks and mortar. They also forced them to do all kinds of hard work in the fields. The Egyptians were not merciful to them in all their hard work. . . .

[22]So the king commanded all his people: "Every time a boy is born to the Hebrews, you must throw him into the Nile River. But let all the girl babies live."

2 [1]There was a man from the family of Levi. He married a woman who was also from the family of Levi. [2]She

became pregnant and gave birth to a son. She saw how wonderful the baby was, and she hid him for three months. [3]But after three months, she was not able to hide the baby any longer. So she got a basket made of reeds and covered it with tar so that it would float. She put the baby in the basket. Then she put the basket among the tall grass at the edge of the Nile River. [4]The baby's sister stood a short distance away. She wanted to see what would happen to him.

[5]Then the daughter of the king of Egypt came to the river. She was going to take a bath. Her servant girls were walking beside the river. She saw the basket in the tall grass. So she sent her slave girl to get it. [6]The king's daughter opened the basket and saw the baby boy. He was crying, and she felt sorry for him. She said, "This is one of the Hebrew babies."

[7]Then the baby's sister asked the king's daughter, "Would you like me to find a Hebrew woman to nurse the baby for you?"

[8]The king's daughter said, "Yes, please." So the girl went and got the baby's own mother.

[9]The king's daughter said to the woman, "Take this baby and nurse him for me. I will pay you." So the woman took her baby and nursed him. [10]After the child had grown older, the woman took him to the king's daughter. She adopted the baby as her own son. The king's daughter named him Moses, because she had pulled him out of the water.

Sometimes heroes are mighty warriors who run out to fight the villains. But sometimes heroes are ordinary girls and boys who dare to help those who can't help themselves—even when it is scary. Miriam was just a slave girl, and the princess was . . . well . . . she was the princess of all Egypt. Just by speaking to her, Miriam could have been beaten—or worse! But she knew that her baby brother needed her help, and she decided to take a chance. She decided to be a hero.

Do you know someone who needs a hero? Maybe it's someone who sits alone at lunch? Or someone who gets picked on or teased? Being that person's friend could be risky. You could end up being the one who gets teased. Are you willing to take the chance? Do you dare to be that person's hero? God hopes that you will be willing to "defend the rights of the poor and suffering" (Psalm 82:3).

HEROES KNOW THAT THEY MUST STAND UP FOR THE WEAK.

MOSES: A RELUCTANT HERO

Though Moses grew up in a palace, he never forgot he was an Israelite. So when he saw an Israelite slave being beaten, he killed the Egyptian slave master. The king then wanted to kill him! Moses escaped to the land of Midian. But God still had a plan for him.

from EXODUS 3:1-4:17

O ne day Moses was taking care of Jethro's sheep. Jethro was the priest of Midian and also Moses' father-in-law. Moses led the sheep to the west side of the desert. He came to Sinai, the mountain of God. ²There the angel of the Lord appeared to Moses in flames of fire coming out of a bush. Moses saw that the bush was on fire, but it was not burning up. ³So Moses said, "I will go closer to this strange thing. How can a bush continue burning without burning up?"

⁴The Lord saw Moses was coming to look at the bush. So God called to him from the bush, "Moses, Moses!"

And Moses said, "Here I am."

⁵Then God said, "Do not come any closer. Take off your sandals. You are standing on holy ground. ⁶I am the God of your ancestors. I am the God of Abraham, the God of Isaac and the God of Jacob." Moses covered his face because he was afraid to look at God.

⁷The Lord said, "I have seen the troubles my people have suffered in Egypt. And I have heard their cries when the Egyptian slave masters hurt them. I am concerned about their pain. ⁸I have come down to save them from the Egyptians. I will bring them out of that land. I will lead them to a good land with lots of room. This is a land where much food grows. This is the land of these people: the Canaanites, Hittites, Amorites, Perizzites, Hivites and Jebusites. ⁹I have heard the cries of the people of Israel. I have seen the way the Egyptians have made life hard for them. ¹⁰So now I am sending you to the king of Egypt. Go! Bring my people, the Israelites, out of Egypt!"

¹¹But Moses said to God, "I am not a great man! Why should I be the one to go to the king and lead the Israelites out of Egypt?"

¹²God said, "I will be with you. This will be the proof that I am sending you: You will lead the people out of Egypt. Then all of you will worship me on this mountain."

¹³Moses said to God, "When I go to the Israelites, I will say to them, 'The God of your fathers sent me to you.' What if the people say, 'What is his name?' What should I tell them?"

¹⁴Then God said to Moses, "I AM WHO I AM. When you go to the people of Israel, tell them, 'I AM sent me to you.'" . . .

4 ¹Then Moses answered, "What if the people of Israel do not believe me or listen to me? What if they say, 'The Lord did not appear to you'?"

²The Lord said to him, "What is that in your hand?"

Moses answered, "It is my walking stick."

³The Lord said, "Throw it on the ground.

So Moses threw it on the ground. And it became a snake. Moses ran from the snake. ⁴But the Lord said to him, "Reach out and grab the snake by its tail." So Moses reached out and took hold of the snake. When he did this, it again became a stick in his hand. ⁵The Lord said, "When this happens, the Israelites will believe that the Lord appeared to you. I am the God of their ancestors. I am the God of Abraham, the God of Isaac and the God of Jacob."

⁶Then the Lord said to Moses, "Put your hand inside your coat. When he took his hand out, it was white with a harmful skin disease.

⁷Then the Lord said, "Now put your hand inside your coat again." So Moses put his hand inside his coat again. When he took it out, his hand was healthy again. It was like the rest of his skin.

⁸Then the Lord said, "The people may not believe you or be convinced by the first miracle. They may believe you when you show them this second miracle. ⁹After these two miracles they still may not believe or listen to you. Then take some water from the Nile River. Pour it on the dry ground. The water will become blood when it touches the ground."

¹⁰But Moses said to the Lord, "But Lord, I am not a skilled speaker. I have never been able to speak well. And now, even after talking to you, I am not a good speaker. I speak slowly and can't find the best words."

¹¹Then the Lord said to him, "Who made man's mouth? And who makes him deaf or not able to speak? Or who gives a man sight or makes him blind? It is I, the Lord. ¹²Now go! I will help you speak. I will tell you what to say."

¹³But Moses said, "Please, Lord, send someone else."

¹⁴The Lord became angry with Moses. He said, "Your brother Aaron, from the family of Levi, is a skilled speaker. He is already coming to meet you. And he will be happy when he sees you. ¹⁵I will tell you what to say. Then you will tell Aaron. I will help both of you know what to say and

do." [16]And Aaron will speak to the people for you. You will tell him what God says. And he will speak for you. [17]Take your walking stick with you. Use it to do the miracles."

Even after Moses saw the miracle of the burning bush, and even after he heard the voice of God, Moses didn't want to be a hero. He had lots of excuses: It would be hard. The king would be mean. He couldn't speak well. But God had an answer for every excuse.

One day, God will ask you to be a hero. He'll ask you to do something new, maybe even something hard. And you might have lots of excuses. But God gives you the same answers that he gave to Moses: "I will be with you," and "I will help . . . you know what to say and do." And God's heroes know that God always keeps his promises!

HEROES DO THEIR VERY BEST FOR GOD!

PHARAOH,
EGYPT'S EVIL
KING, REFUSES
TO LET GOD'S
PEOPLE GO.

EGYPT'S EVIL KING

The king of Egypt made life for the Israelites harder and harder. They cried out to God for help, and God sent Moses to the king with a message. But would such an evil king ever let God's people go?

from EXODUS 7:14-12:42

The Lord said to Moses, "The king is being stubborn. He refuses to let the people go. ¹⁵In the morning the king will go out to the Nile River. Go meet him by the edge of the river. Take with you the walking stick that became a snake. ¹⁶Tell him this: The Lord, the God of the Hebrews, sent me to you. He said, 'Let my people go worship me in the desert.'

Until now you have not listened. ¹⁷This is what the Lord says: 'This is how you will know that I am the Lord. I will strike the water of the Nile River with this stick in my hand. And the water will change into blood. ¹⁸Then the fish in the Nile will die, and the river will begin to stink. And the Egyptians will not be able to drink the water from the Nile.'"

¹⁹The Lord said to Moses, "Tell Aaron to stretch the walking stick in his hand over the rivers, canals, ponds and pools in Egypt. The water will become blood everywhere in Egypt. There even will be blood in the wooden buckets and stone jars."

²⁰So Moses and Aaron did just as the Lord had commanded. Aaron raised his walking stick and struck the water in the Nile River. He did this in front of the king and his officers. So all the water in the Nile changed into blood. ²¹The fish in the Nile died, and the river began to stink. So the Egyptians could not drink water from it. Blood was everywhere in the land of Egypt.

²²Using their tricks, their magicians of Egypt did the same thing. So the king was stubborn and refused to listen to Moses and Aaron. This happened just as the Lord had said. ²³The king turned and went into his palace. He ignored what Moses and Aaron had done. ²⁴The Egyptians could not drink the water from the Nile. So all of them dug along the bank of the river. They were looking for water to drink.

The king still refused to let the Hebrew people go. So God sent plagues of frogs, gnats, and flies. All the Egyptian farm animals died from a terrible disease. Boils covered the people. Hail destroyed many of the Egyptian crops, and swarms of locusts ate the rest. Darkness covered the entire land of Egypt. But in the land of Goshen, where the Hebrews lived, all was well. Still, after all these terrible plagues, the king would not let the Hebrew people go. Then came the most terrible plague of all.

11 [1]Now the Lord told Moses, "I have one more way to punish the king and the people of Egypt. After this, the king will send all of you away from Egypt. When he does, he will force you to leave completely. [2]Tell the men and women of Israel to ask their neighbors for things made of silver and gold" [3]The Lord had caused the Egyptians to respect the Israelites. The king's officers and the Egyptian people already considered Moses to be a great man.

[4]So Moses said to the king, "This is what the Lord says: 'About midnight tonight I will go through all Egypt. [5]Every firstborn son in the land of Egypt will die. . . . [7]Then you will know that the Lord treats Israel differently from Egypt.'" . . . [8]Then Moses very angrily left the king. . . .

12

²⁹At midnight the Lord killed all the firstborn sons in the land of Egypt. The firstborn of the king, who sat on the throne, died. Even the firstborn of the prisoner in jail died. Also all the firstborn farm animals died. ³⁰The king, his officers and all the Egyptians got up during the night. Someone had died in every house. So there was loud crying everywhere in Egypt.

³¹During the night the king called for Moses and Aaron. He said to them, "Get up and leave my people. You and your people may do as you have asked. Go and worship the Lord. ³²Take all of your sheep and cattle as you have asked. Go. And also bless me." ³³The Egyptians also asked the Israelites to hurry and leave. They said, "If you don't leave, we will all die!"

³⁴The people of Israel took their dough before the yeast was added. They wrapped the bowls for making dough in clothing and carried them on their shoulders. ³⁵The people of Israel did what Moses told them to do. They asked their Egyptian neighbors for things made of silver and gold and for clothing. ³⁶The Lord caused the Egyptians to think well of the Israelites. So the Israelites took rich gifts from the Egyptians.

³⁷The Israelites traveled from Rameses to Succoth. There were about 600,000 men walking. This does not include the women and children. ³⁸Many other people who were not Israelites went with them. A large number of sheep,

goats and cattle went with them. ³⁹The Israelites used the dough they had brought out of Egypt. They baked loaves of bread without yeast. The dough had no yeast in it because they had been rushed out of Egypt. So they had no time to get food ready for their trip.

⁴⁰The people of Israel had lived in Egypt for 430 years. ⁴¹On the day the 430 years ended, the Lord's divisions of people left Egypt. ⁴²That night the Lord kept watch to bring them out of Egypt.

The Egyptian king was a true villain. Even though his own people suffered from frogs, locusts, boils, gnats, flies, and hail, he would not let God's people go. The hard-hearted king would not listen until his own first-born child died. If only he had listened to God, but he did not, and so his heart was broken.

Listening to God is the first step toward being a hero. God only wants the best for you. When you listen to him and obey him, he will bless your life. But when you don't listen to God, your heart can end up broken.

Listening isn't hard. All it takes is a little time, a quiet spot, and a heart that is willing to listen to what God has to say.

HEROES LISTEN TO GOD.

MOSES HOLDS HIS STAFF OVER THE WATERS AS GOD PARTS THE RED SEA.

Moses Leads the People

The Egyptian king told the Israelite slaves to leave Egypt and never return. But what happened to the Israelites when the king changed his mind?

from EXODUS 14:5-31

The king of Egypt was told that the people of Israel had already left. Then he and his officers changed their minds about them. They said, "What have we done? We have let the people of Israel leave. We have lost our slaves!" ⁶So the king prepared his war chariot and took his army with him. ⁷He took 600 of his best chariots. He also took all the other chariots of Egypt. Each chariot had an officer in it. ⁸The Lord made the king of Egypt stubborn. So he chased the Israelites, who were leaving victoriously. ⁹The king of Egypt came with his horses, chariot drivers and army. And they chased the Israelites. They caught up with the Israelites while they were camped by the Red Sea. This was near Pi Hahiroth and Baal Zephon.

¹⁰The Israelites saw the king and his army coming after them. They were very frightened and cried to the Lord for help. ¹¹They said to Moses, "What have you done to us? Why did you bring us out of Egypt to die in the desert? There were plenty of graves for us in Egypt. ¹²We told you in Egypt, 'Let us alone! Let us stay and serve the Egyptians.' Now we will die in the desert."

¹³But Moses answered, "Don't be afraid! Stand still and see the Lord save you today. You will never see these Egyptians again after today. ¹⁴You will only need to remain calm. The Lord will fight for you."

¹⁵Then the Lord said to Moses, "Why are you crying out to me? Command the people of Israel to start moving. ¹⁶Raise your walking stick and hold it over the sea. The sea will split. Then the people can cross the sea on dry land. ¹⁷I have made the Egyptians stubborn so they will chase the Israelites. But I will be honored when I defeat the king and all of his chariot drivers and chariots. ¹⁸I will defeat

the king, his chariot drivers and chariots. Then Egypt will know that I am the Lord."

[19]The angel of God usually traveled in front of Israel's army. Now the angel of God moved behind them. Also, the pillar of cloud moved from in front of the people and stood behind them. [20]So the cloud came between the Egyptians and the people of Israel. The cloud made it dark for the Egyptians. But it gave light to the Israelites. So the cloud kept the two armies apart all night.

[21]Moses held his hand over the sea. All that night the Lord drove back the sea with a strong east wind. And so he made the sea become dry ground. The water was split. [22]And the Israelites went through the sea on dry land. A wall of water was on both sides.

[23]Then all the king's horses, chariots and chariot drivers followed them into the sea. [24]Between two and six o'clock in the morning, the Lord looked down from the pillar of cloud and fire at the Egyptian army. He made them panic. [25]He kept the wheels of the chariots from turning. This made it hard to drive the chariots. The Egyptians shouted, "Let's get away from the Israelites! The Lord is fighting for them and against us Egyptians."

[26]Then the Lord told Moses, "Hold your hand over the sea. Then the water will come back over the Egyptians, their chariots and chariot drivers." [27]So Moses raised his hand over the sea. And at dawn the water became deep again. The Egyptians were trying to run from it. But the Lord swept them away into the sea. [28]The water became

deep again. It covered the chariots and chariot drivers. So all the king's army that had followed the Israelites into the sea was covered. Not one of them survived.

²⁹But the people of Israel crossed the sea on dry land. There was a wall of water on their right and on their left. ³⁰So that day the Lord saved the Israelites from the Egyptians. And the Israelites saw the Egyptians lying dead on the seashore. ³¹When the people of Israel saw the great power that the Lord had used against the Egyptians, they feared the Lord. And they trusted the Lord and his servant Moses.

The Israelites were terrified, and they were trapped—with the Red Sea on one side and the evil king's army on the other. They didn't know what to do! But Moses did. When he saw trouble coming, he trusted God. He told the people, "Don't be afraid! Stand still and see the Lord save you today."

So when you don't know what to do, trust God to take care of you. Be a hero of faith . . . and know that God will never let you down.

HEROES KNOW THEY CAN ALWAYS COUNT ON GOD.

RAHAB BELIEVES

When Moses died, God made Joshua the new leader of his people. It was Joshua's job to lead the Israelites into the Promised Land. Many battles would have to be fought, and the first was against the mighty city of Jericho, where there lived a most unlikely hero.

from JOSHUA 1:1-2:24

After Moses died, the Lord said to Joshua, ²"My servant Moses is dead. Now you and all these people go across the Jordan River. Go into the land I am giving to the people of Israel. ³I promised Moses I would give you this land. So I will give you every place you go in the land." . . .

¹⁰So Joshua gave orders to the officers of the people. He said, ¹¹"Go through the camp and tell the people, 'Get your supplies ready. Three days from now you will cross the Jordan River. You will go and take the land the Lord your God is giving you.'" . . .

2 ¹Joshua son of Nun secretly sent out two spies from Acacia. Joshua said to them, "Go and look at the land. Look closely at the city of Jericho."

So the men went to Jericho. They went to the house of a prostitute and stayed there. This woman's name was Rahab.

²Someone told the king of Jericho, "Some men from Israel have come here tonight. They are spying out the land."

³So the king of Jericho sent this message to Rahab: "Bring out the men who came to you and entered your house. They have come to spy out our whole land."

⁴Now the woman had hidden the two men. She said, "They did come here. But I didn't know where they came from. ⁵In the evening, when it was time to close the city gate, they left. I don't know where they went. Go quickly. Maybe you can catch them." ⁶(But the woman had taken the men up to the roof. She had hidden them there under stalks of flax. She had spread the flax out there to dry.) ⁷So

the king's men went out looking for the spies from Israel. They went to the places where people cross the Jordan River. The city gate was closed just after the king's men left the city.

[8]The spies were ready to sleep for the night. So Rahab went to the roof and talked to them. [9]She said, "I know the Lord has given this land to your people. You frighten us very much. Everyone living in this land is terribly afraid of you. [10]We are afraid because we have heard how the Lord helped you. We heard how he dried up the Red Sea when you came out of Egypt. We heard how you destroyed Sihon and Og. They were the two Amorite kings who lived east of the Jordan. [11]When we heard this, we became very frightened. Now our men are afraid to fight you. This is because the Lord your God rules the heavens above and the earth below! [12]So now, make me a promise before the Lord. Promise that you will show kindness to my family just as I showed you kindness. Give me some proof that you will do this. [13]Promise me you will allow my family to live. Save my father, mother, brothers, sisters and all of their families from death."

[14]The men agreed. They said, "We will trade our lives for your lives. Don't tell anyone what we are doing. When the Lord gives us our land, we will be kind to you. You may trust us."

[15]The house Rahab lived in was built on the city wall. So she used a rope to let the men down through a window. [16]She said to them, "Go into the hills. The king's men will

not find you there. Hide there for three days. After the king's men return, you may go on your way."

[17]The men said to her, "You must do as we say. If not, we cannot be responsible for keeping our promise. [18]You are using a red rope to help us escape. When we return to this land, you must tie it in the window through which you let us down. Bring your father, mother, brothers and all your family into your house. [19]We can keep everyone safe who stays in this house. If anyone in your house is hurt, we will be responsible. If anyone goes out of your house and is killed, it is his own fault. We cannot be responsible for him. [20]But you must not tell anyone about this agreement. If you do, we are free from it."

[21]Rahab answered, "I agree to this." So she sent them away, and they left. Then she tied the red rope in the window.

[22]The men left and went into the hills. There they stayed for three days. The king's men looked for them all along the road. But after three days, the king's men returned to the city without finding them. [23]Then the two men started back to Joshua. They left the hills and crossed the river. They went to Joshua son of Nun and told him everything that had happened to them. [24]They said to Joshua, "The Lord surely has given us all of the land. All the people in that land are terribly afraid of us."

When the battle of Jericho was fought, Joshua sent the two spies back to Rahab to make sure that she and all her family were kept safe. They were saved because Rahab believed that "God rules the heavens above and the earth below!"

When you choose to believe in God and in his love and power, he will save you too. Zephaniah 3:17 promises, "The Lord your God is with you. The mighty One will save you. The Lord will be happy with you."

HEROES BELIEVE IN THE ONE TRUE GOD.

JOSHUA FOLLOWS GOD'S PLAN TO DEFEAT JERICHO.

Joshua Obeys

A great wall surrounded the mighty city of Jericho. In order to conquer the city, Joshua and the Israelite people had to get through that wall. It did not seem possible, but God had a most unusual plan.

from JOSHUA 5:13-6:27

Joshua was near Jericho. He looked up and saw a man standing in front of him. The man had a sword in his hand. Joshua went to him and asked, "Are you a friend or an enemy?"

¹⁴The man answered, "I am neither one. I have come as the commander of the Lord's army."

Then Joshua bowed facedown on the ground. He asked, "Does my master have a command for me, his servant?"

[15]The commander of the Lord's army answered, "Take off your sandals. The place where you are standing is holy." So Joshua did.

6 [1]Now the people of Jericho were afraid because the Israelites were near. So they closed the city gates and guarded them. No one went into the city. And no one came out.

[2]Then the Lord spoke to Joshua. He said, "Look, I have given you Jericho, its king and all its fighting men. [3]March around the city with your army one time every day. Do this for six days. [4]Have seven priests carry trumpets made from horns of male sheep. Tell them to march in front of the Holy Box. On the seventh day march around the city seven times. On that day tell the priests to blow the trumpets as they march. [5]They will make one long blast on the trumpets. When you hear that sound, have all the people give a loud shout. Then the walls of the city will fall. And the people will go straight into the city."

[6]So Joshua son of Nun called the priests together. He said to them, "Carry the Box of the Agreement with the Lord. Tell seven priests to carry trumpets and march in front of it." [7]Then Joshua ordered the people, "Now go! March around the city. The soldiers with weapons should march in front of the Box of the Agreement with the Lord."

[8]So Joshua finished speaking to the people. Then the seven priests began marching before the Lord.

They carried the seven trumpets and blew them as they marched. The priests carrying the Box of the Agreement with the Lord followed them. ⁹The soldiers with weapons marched in front of the priests. And armed men walked behind the Holy Box. They were blowing their trumpets. ¹⁰But Joshua had told the people not to give a war cry. He said, "Don't shout. Don't say a word until the day I tell you. Then shout!" ¹¹So Joshua had the Holy Box of the Lord carried around the city one time. Then they went back to camp for the night.

¹²Early the next morning Joshua got up. And the priests carried the Holy Box of the Lord again. ¹³The seven priests carried the seven trumpets. They marched in front of the Holy Box of the Lord, blowing their trumpets. The soldiers with weapons marched in front of them. Other soldiers walked behind the Holy Box of the Lord. All this time the priests were blowing their trumpets. ¹⁴So on the second day they marched around the city one time. Then they went back to camp. They did this every day for six days.

¹⁵On the seventh day they got up at dawn. They marched around the city seven times. They marched just as they had on the days before. But on that day they marched around the city seven times. ¹⁶The seventh time around the priests blew their trumpets. Then Joshua gave the command: "Now, shout! The Lord has given you this city! ¹⁷The city and everything in it are to be destroyed as an offering to the Lord. Only Rahab the prostitute and everyone in her house should remain alive. They must not be killed. This is

because Rahab hid the two spies we sent out. [18]Don't take any of the things that are to be destroyed as an offering to the Lord. If you take them and bring them into our camp, then you yourselves will be destroyed. You will also bring trouble to all of Israel. [19]All the silver and gold and things made from bronze and iron belong to the Lord. They must be saved for him."

[20]When the priests blew the trumpets, the people shouted. At the sound of the trumpets and the people's shout, the walls fell. And everyone ran straight into the city. So the Israelites defeated that city. [21]They completely destroyed every living thing in the city. They killed men and women, young and old. They killed cattle, sheep and donkeys.

[22]Joshua spoke to the two men who had spied out the land. Joshua said, "Go into the prostitute's house. Bring her out. And bring out all the people who are with her. Do this because of the promise you made to her." [23]So the two men went into the house and brought out Rahab. They also brought out her father, mother, brothers and all those with her. They put all of her family in a safe place outside the camp of Israel.

[24]Then Israel burned the whole city and everything in it. But they did not burn the things made from silver, gold, bronze and iron. These were saved for the Lord. [25]Joshua saved Rahab the prostitute, her family and all who were with her. He let them live. This was because Rahab had helped the men he had sent to spy out Jericho. Rahab still lives among the Israelites today. . . .

²⁷So the Lord was with Joshua. And Joshua became famous through all the land.

Joshua and the Israelites were ready for a fight. But God didn't ask them to fight; he asked them to march. It didn't make sense, but Joshua obeyed God, because that's what heroes do. And God's people won because it was God's perfect plan.

Sometimes God asks you to do things that don't make sense: "Love your enemies. Do good to those who hate you. Ask God to bless those who say bad things to you" (Luke 6:27–28). Often that's not what those in this world say to do, but that's what God wants you to do.

HEROES OBEY GOD . . . EVEN WHEN THEY DON'T UNDERSTAND.

GIDEON WATCHES AS THE LORD DEFEATS THE ARMY OF MIDIAN.

GIDEON: GOD'S MIGHTY WARRIOR

In the times of the judges, Israel would sometimes worship false idols, forgetting the One True God. Because Israel left God and his protection, they were attacked by their enemies. But when Israel remembered God and cried out to him for help, God raised up a judge to save his people.

from JUDGES 6:1–7:22

Again the people of Israel did what the Lord said was wrong. So for seven years the Lord let the people of

Midian rule Israel. [2]The Midianites were very powerful and were cruel to the Israelites. So the Israelites made hiding places in the mountains. They also hid in caves and safe places. [3]Whenever the Israelites planted crops, the Midianites, Amalekites and other peoples from the east would come and attack them. [4]These people camped in the land. And they destroyed the crops that the Israelites had planted. They did this as far as the land near Gaza. The people left nothing for Israel to eat. They left them no sheep, cattle or donkeys. . . .

[11]Gideon was separating some wheat from the chaff in a winepress. Gideon did this to keep the wheat from the Midianites. [12]The angel of the Lord appeared to Gideon and said, "The Lord is with you, mighty warrior!"

[13]Then Gideon said, "Pardon me, sir. If the Lord is with us, why are we having so many troubles? Our ancestors told us he did miracles. They told us the Lord brought them out of Egypt. But now he has left us. He has allowed the Midianites to defeat us."

[14]The Lord turned to Gideon and said, "You have the strength to save the people of Israel. Go and save them from the Midianites. I am the one who is sending you."

[15]But Gideon answered, "Pardon me, Lord. How can I save Israel? My family group is the weakest in Manasseh. And I am the least important member of my family."

[16]The Lord answered him, "I will be with you. It will seem as if you are fighting only one man."

[17]Then Gideon said to the Lord, "If you are pleased with me, give me proof. Show me that it is really you talking with me. [18]Please wait here. Do not go away until I come back to you. Let me bring my offering and set it in front of you."

And the Lord said, "I will wait until you come back."

[19]So Gideon went in and cooked a young goat. He also took about 20 quarts of flour and made bread without yeast. Then he put the meat into a basket. And he put the broth from the boiled meat into a pot. He brought out the meat, the broth and the bread without yeast. He brought the food to the angel of the Lord. Gideon gave it to him under the oak tree.

[20]The angel of God said to Gideon, "Put the meat and the bread without yeast on that rock over there. Then pour the broth on them." And Gideon did as he was told. [21]The angel of the Lord had a stick in his hand. He touched the meat and the bread with the end of the stick. Then fire jumped up from the rock! The meat and the bread were completely burned up! And the angel of the Lord disappeared! [22]Then Gideon understood he had been talking to the angel of the Lord. So Gideon cried, "Lord God! I have seen the angel of the Lord face to face!"

[23]But the Lord said to Gideon, "Calm down! Don't be afraid! You will not die!"

[24]So Gideon built an altar there to worship the Lord. Gideon named the altar The Lord Is Peace. . . .

³³All the Midianites, the Amalekites and other peoples from the east joined together. They came across the Jordan River and camped in the Valley of Jezreel. ³⁴But the Spirit of the Lord entered Gideon! Gideon blew a trumpet to call the Abiezrites to follow him. ³⁵He sent messengers to all of Manasseh. The people of Manasseh were called to follow Gideon. Gideon also sent messengers to the people of Asher, Zebulun and Naphtali. They also went up to meet Gideon and his men.

³⁶Then Gideon said to God, "You said you would help me save Israel. ³⁷I will put some wool on the threshing floor. Let there be dew only on the wool. But let all of the ground be dry. Then I will know what you said is true. I will know that you will use me to save Israel." ³⁸And that is just what happened. Gideon got up early the next morning and squeezed the wool. He got a full bowl of water from the wool.

³⁹Then Gideon said to God, "Don't be angry with me. Let me ask just one more thing. Please let me make one more test. Let the wool be dry while the ground around it gets wet with dew." ⁴⁰That night God did that very thing. Just the wool was dry, but the ground around it was wet with dew.

7 ¹Early in the morning Jerub-Baal and all his men set up their camp at the spring of Harod. (Jerub-Baal is also called Gideon.) The Midianites were camped north of them. The Midianites were camped in the valley at the bottom of

the hill called Moreh. ²Then the Lord said to Gideon, "You have too many men to defeat the Midianites. I don't want the Israelites to brag that they saved themselves. ³So now, announce to the people, 'Anyone who is afraid may leave Mount Gilead. He may go back home.'" And 22,000 men went back home. But 10,000 remained.

⁴Then the Lord said to Gideon, "There are still too many men. Take the men down to the water, and I will test them for you there." . . .

⁵So Gideon led the men down to the water. There the Lord said to him, "Separate them. Those who drink water by lapping it up like a dog will be in one group. Those who bend down to drink will be in the other group." ⁶There were 300 men who used their hands to bring water to their mouths. They lapped it as a dog does. All the rest got down on their knees to drink.

⁷Then the Lord said to Gideon, "I will save you, using the 300 men who lapped the water. And I will allow you to defeat Midian. Let all the other men go to their homes." ⁸So Gideon sent the rest of Israel to their homes. But he kept 300 men. He took the jars and the trumpets of those who went home.

Now the camp of Midian was in the valley below Gideon. ⁹That night the Lord spoke to Gideon. He said, "Get up. Go down and attack the camp of the Midianites. I will allow you to defeat them. ¹⁰But if you are afraid to go down, take your servant Purah with you. ¹¹When you come to the camp of Midian, you will hear what they are saying. Then you will not be afraid to attack the camp."

[11]So Gideon and his servant Purah went down to the edge of the enemy camp. . . .

[13]When Gideon came to the enemy camp, he heard a man talking. That man was telling his friend about a dream. He was saying, "Listen, I dreamed that a loaf of barley bread rolled into the camp of Midian. It hit the tent so hard that the tent turned over and fell flat!"

[14]The man's friend said, "Your dream is about the sword of Gideon son of Joash, a man of Israel. God will let Gideon defeat Midian and the whole army!"

[15]When Gideon heard about the dream and what it meant, he worshiped God. Then Gideon went back to the camp of Israel. He called out to them, "Get up! The Lord has defeated the army of Midian for you!" [16]Then Gideon divided the 300 men into three groups. He gave each man a trumpet and an empty jar. A burning torch was inside each jar. . . .

[19]So Gideon and the 100 men with him came to the edge of the enemy camp. They came just after the enemy had changed guards. It was during the middle watch of the night. Then Gideon and his men blew their trumpets and smashed their jars. [20]All three groups of Gideon's men blew their trumpets and smashed their jars. They held the torches in their left hands and the trumpets in their right hands. Then they shouted, "A sword for the Lord and for Gideon!" [21]Each of Gideon's men stayed in his place around the camp. But inside the camp, the men of Midian began shouting and running away.

[22]When Gideon's 300 men blew their trumpets, the

Lord caused all the men of Midian to fight each other with their swords! The enemy army ran away.

When the angel of the Lord appeared and called him a mighty warrior, Gideon wasn't feeling like one. At that moment, he was hiding in a sort of hole in the ground. Yet God called him a mighty warrior. How could that be? The answer is in the first few words the angel spoke: "The Lord is with you" (Judges 6:12).

When God is with you, you can defeat any enemy. Whether it's an invading army, a playground bully, or your own bad habit that you need to conquer, God will be right by your side. He will guide you to the right choices and the right people to help you. God doesn't just want you to be a hero; he will help you become a hero.

GOD CAN MAKE A HERO OUT OF ANYONE WHO BELIEVES.

DELILAH HELPS
THE PHILISTINES
CAPTURE
SAMSON.

DELILAH BETRAYS SAMSON

The Philistines were the enemies of God's people. God raised up Samson, a mighty warrior, to defend his people from the Philistines. But one day, Samson trusted in the wrong person—himself!

from JUDGES 16:4-30

Samson fell in love with a woman named Delilah. She lived in the Valley of Sorek. [5]The kings of the Philistines went to Delilah. They said, "Try to find out what makes Samson so strong. Try to trick him into telling you. Find out how we could capture him and tie him up. Then we will be able to control him. If you do this, each one of us will give you 28 pounds of silver."

⁶So Delilah said to Samson, "Tell me why you are so strong. How could someone tie you up and take control of you?"

⁷Samson answered, "Someone would have to tie me up. He would have to use seven new bowstrings that have not been dried. If he did that, I would be as weak as any other man."

⁸Then the kings of the Philistines brought seven new bowstrings to Delilah. They had not been dried. She tied Samson with them. ⁹Some men were hiding in another room. Delilah said to Samson, "Samson, the Philistines are about to capture you!" But Samson easily broke the bowstrings. They broke like pieces of string burned in a fire. So the Philistines did not find out the secret of Samson's strength.

¹⁰Then Delilah said to Samson, "You've made me look foolish. You lied to me. Please tell me. How could someone tie you up?"

¹¹Samson said, "They would have to tie me with new ropes that have not been used before. Then I would become as weak as any other man."

¹²So Delilah took new ropes and tied Samson. Some men were hiding in another room. Then she called out to him, "Samson, the Philistines are about to capture you!" But he broke the ropes as easily as if they were threads.

[13]Then Delilah said to Samson, "Until now, you have made me look foolish. You have lied to me. Tell me how someone could tie you up."

He said, "Use the loom. Weave the seven braids of my hair into the cloth. Tighten it with a pin. Then I will become as weak as any other man."

Then Samson went to sleep. So Delilah wove the seven braids of his hair into the cloth. [14]Then she fastened it with a pin.

Again she called out to him, "Samson, the Philistines are about to capture you!" Samson woke up and pulled up the pin and the loom with the cloth.

[15]Then Delilah said to him, "How can you say, 'I love you,' when you don't even trust me? This is the third time you have made me look foolish. You haven't told me the secret of your great strength." [16]She kept bothering Samson about his secret day after day. He became so tired of it he felt he was going to die!

[17]So he told her everything. He said, "I have never had my hair cut. I have been set apart to God as a Nazirite since I was born. If someone shaved my head, then I would lose my strength. I would become as weak as any other man."

[18]Delilah saw that he had told her everything sincerely. So she sent a message to the kings of the Philistines. She said, "Come back one more time. He has told me everything." So the kings of the Philistines came back to Delilah. They brought the silver they had promised to give her. [19]Delilah got Samson to go to sleep. He was lying in her lap. Then she

called in a man to shave off the seven braids of Samson's hair. In this way she began to make him weak. And Samson's strength left him.

[20]Then she called out to him, "Samson, the Philistines are about to capture you!"

He woke up and thought, "I'll get loose as I did before and shake myself free." But he did not know that the Lord had left him.

[21]Then the Philistines captured Samson. They tore out his eyes. And they took him down to Gaza. They put bronze chains on him. They put him in prison and made him grind grain. [22]But his hair began to grow again.

[23]The kings of the Philistines gathered to celebrate. They were going to offer a great sacrifice to their god Dagon. They said, "Our god has given us Samson our enemy." . . .

[25]The people were having a good time at the celebration. They said, "Bring Samson out to perform for us." So they brought Samson from the prison. He performed for them. They made him stand between the pillars of the temple of Dagon. [26]A servant was holding his hand. Samson said to him, "Let me feel the pillars that hold up the temple. I want to lean against them." [27]Now the temple was full of men and women. All the kings of the Philistines were there. There were about 3,000 men and women on the roof. They watched Samson perform. [28]Then Samson prayed to the Lord. He said, "Lord God, remember me. God, please give me strength one more time. Let me

pay these Philistines back for putting out my two eyes!" [29]Then Samson held the two center pillars of the temple. These two pillars supported the whole temple. He braced himself between the two pillars. His right hand was on one, and his left hand was on the other. [30]Samson said, "Let me die with these Philistines!" Then he pushed as hard as he could. And the temple fell on the kings and all the people in it. So Samson killed more of the Philistines when he died than when he was alive.

Samson was the strongest man alive, but he trusted in his own strength more than God's. Delilah used that to betray Samson and turn him over to his enemies.

When you trust in your own strength—or abilities or talents—rather than remembering they are gifts from God, that is when you are actually the weakest. When you use your talents to show off, instead of to point people to God, that is when someone can betray you. "Every good action and every perfect gift is from God" (James 1:17). Pray that he will help you use your gifts wisely—that's what a real hero would do.

REAL HEROES KNOW THAT TRUE STRENGTH COMES FROM GOD.

RUTH GATHERS GRAIN IN THE FIELDS BELONGING TO BOAZ.

Ruth Is Faithful

> *Ruth had to decide whether to stay in the country she had always lived in, with the people she knew, or go to a strange new land to be with someone who needed her.*

from RUTH 1:1-4:17

Long ago the judges ruled Israel. During their rule, there was a time in the land when there was not enough food to eat. A man named Elimelech left Bethlehem in Judah and moved to the country of Moab. He took his wife and his two sons with him. His wife was named Naomi, and his two sons were named Mahlon and Kilion. These people were from the Ephrathah district around

Bethlehem in Judah. The family traveled to Moab and lived there.

³Later, Naomi's husband, Elimelech, died. So only Naomi and her two sons were left. ⁴These sons married women from Moab. The name of one wife was Orpah. The name of the other wife was Ruth. Naomi and her sons lived in Moab about ten years. ⁵Then Mahlon and Kilion also died. So Naomi was left alone without her husband or her two sons.

⁶While Naomi was in Moab, she heard that the Lord had taken care of his people. He had given food to them in Judah. So Naomi got ready to leave Moab and go back home. The wives of Naomi's sons also got ready to go with her. ⁷So they left the place where they had lived. And they started back on the way to the land of Judah. ⁸But Naomi said to her two daughters-in-law, "Go back home. Each of you go to your own mother's house. You have been very kind to me and to my sons who are now dead. I hope the Lord will also be kind to you in the same way. ⁹I hope the Lord will give you another home and a new husband."

Then Naomi kissed the women. And they began to cry out loud. ¹⁰Her daughters-in-law said to her, "No. We will go with you to your people."

¹¹But Naomi said, "My daughters, go back to your own homes. Why do you want to go with me? I cannot give birth to more sons to give you new husbands. ¹²So go back to your own homes. . . . ¹³My life is much too sad for you to share. This is because the Lord is against me!"

[14]The women cried together again. Then Orpah kissed Naomi good-bye, but Ruth held on to her.

[15]Naomi said, "Look, your sister-in-law is going back to her own people and her own gods. Go back with her."

[16]But Ruth said, "Don't ask me to leave you! Don't beg me not to follow you! Every place you go, I will go. Every place you live, I will live. Your people will be my people. Your God will be my God. [17]And where you die, I will die. And there I will be buried. I ask the Lord to punish me terribly if I do not keep this promise: Only death will separate us."

[18]Naomi saw that Ruth had made up her mind to go with her. So Naomi stopped arguing with her. [19]Naomi and Ruth went on until they came to the town of Bethlehem. When the two women entered Bethlehem, all the people became very excited. The women of the town said, "Is this Naomi?"

[20]But Naomi told the people, "Don't call me Naomi. Call me Mara, because God All-Powerful has made my life very sad." . . .

[22]So Naomi and her daughter-in-law Ruth, the woman from Moab, came back from Moab. They came to Bethlehem at the beginning of the barley harvest.

2 [1]Now there was a rich man living in Bethlehem whose name was Boaz. Boaz was one of Naomi's close relatives from Elimelech's family. [2]One day Ruth, the woman from Moab, said to Naomi, "Let me go to the fields. Maybe someone will be kind and let me gather the grain he leaves in his field."

Naomi said, "Go, my daughter."

[3]So Ruth went to the fields. She followed the workers who were cutting the grain. And she gathered the grain that they had left. It just so happened that the field belonged to Boaz. He was a close relative from Elimelech's family. . . .

[5]Boaz spoke to his servant who was in charge of the workers. He asked, "Whose girl is that?"

[6]The servant answered, "She is the Moabite woman who came with Naomi from the country of Moab. [7]She said, 'Please let me follow the workers and gather the grain that they leave on the ground.' She came and has remained here. From morning until just now, she has stopped only a few moments to rest in the shelter."

[8]Then Boaz said to Ruth, "Listen, my daughter. Stay here in my field to gather grain for yourself. Do not go to any other person's field. Continue following behind my women workers. [9]Watch to see which fields they go to and follow them. I have warned the young men not to bother you. When you are thirsty, you may go and drink. Take water from the water jugs that the servants have filled."

[10]Then Ruth bowed low with her face to the ground. She said to Boaz, "I am a stranger. Why have you been so kind to notice me?"

[11]Boaz answered her, "I know about all the help you

have given to Naomi, your mother-in-law. You helped her even after your husband died. You left your father and mother and your own country. You came to this nation where you did not know anyone. ¹²The Lord will reward you for all you have done. You will be paid in full by the Lord, the God of Israel. You have come to him as a little bird finds shelter under the wings of its mother."

¹³Then Ruth said, "You are very kind to me, sir. You have said kind words to me, your servant." . . .

¹⁴At mealtime Boaz told Ruth, "Come here! Eat some of our bread. Here, dip your bread in our vinegar."

So Ruth sat down with the workers. Boaz gave her some roasted grain. Ruth ate until she was full, and there was some food left over. ¹⁵Ruth rose and went back to work. Then Boaz told his servants, "Let her gather even around the bundles of grain. Don't tell her to go away. ¹⁶Drop some full heads of grain for her. Let her gather that grain, and don't tell her to stop."

¹⁷So Ruth gathered grain in the field until evening. Then she separated the grain from the chaff. There was about one-half bushel of barley. ¹⁸Ruth carried the grain into town. And her mother-in-law saw what she had gathered. Ruth also gave her the food that was left over from lunch.

¹⁹Naomi asked her, "Where did you gather all this grain today? Where did you work? Blessed be the man who noticed you!"

Ruth told her about whose field she had worked in. She said, "The man I worked with today is named Boaz."

[20]Naomi told her daughter-in-law, "The Lord bless him! The Lord still continues to be kind to all people—the living and the dead!" Then Naomi told Ruth, "Boaz is one of our close relatives, one who will take care of us." . . .

[22]Then Naomi said to her daughter-in-law Ruth, "It is good for you to continue working with his women servants. If you work in another field, someone might hurt you." [23]So Ruth continued working closely with the women servants of Boaz. She gathered grain until the barley harvest was finished. She also worked there through the end of the wheat harvest. And Ruth continued to live with Naomi, her mother-in-law.

3 [1]Then Naomi, Ruth's mother-in-law, said to her, "My daughter, I must find a suitable home for you. That would be good for you. [2]Now Boaz is our close relative. You worked with his women servants. Tonight he will be working at the threshing floor. [3]Go wash yourself and put on perfume. Change your clothes, and go down to the threshing floor. But don't let him see you until he has finished eating and drinking. [4]Then he will lie down. Watch him so you will know the place where he lies down. Go there and lift the cover off his feet and lie down. He will tell you what you should do."

[5]Then Ruth answered, "I will do everything you say."

[6]So Ruth went down to the threshing floor. She did all her mother-in-law told her to do. . . .

[8]About midnight Boaz woke up suddenly and rolled over. He was startled! There was a woman lying near his feet! [9]Boaz asked, "Who are you?"

She said, "I am Ruth, your servant girl. Spread your cover over me because you are the one who is to take care of me."

¹⁰Then Boaz said, "The Lord bless you, my daughter. Your kindness to me is greater than the kindness you showed to Naomi in the beginning. You didn't look for a young man to marry, either rich or poor. ¹¹Now, my daughter, don't be afraid. I will do everything you ask. All the people in our town know you are a very good woman." . . .

¹⁶Ruth went to the home of her mother-in-law. And Naomi asked, "How did you do, my daughter?"

So Ruth told Naomi everything that Boaz did for her. ¹⁷She said, "Boaz gave me these six portions of barley. He said, 'You must not go home without a gift for your mother-in-law.'"

¹⁸Naomi answered, "Ruth, my daughter, wait until you hear what happens. Boaz will not rest until he has finished doing what he should do this day." . . .

4 ¹³So Boaz took Ruth and married her. The Lord let her become pregnant, and she gave birth to a son. ¹⁴The women told Naomi, "Praise the Lord who gave you this grandson. And may he become famous in Israel. ¹⁵He will give you new life. And he will take care of you in your old

age. This happened because of your daughter-in-law. She loves you. And she is better for you than seven sons. She has given birth to your grandson."

[16]Naomi took the boy, held him in her arms and cared for him. [17]The neighbors gave the boy his name. These women said, "This boy was born for Naomi." The neighbors named him Obed. Obed was Jesse's father. And Jesse was the father of David.

Ruth was a quiet hero. It would have been easier to stay in her own country, with her own family. But Ruth loved Naomi, and she knew that Naomi needed her help. So Ruth left everything she knew and traveled far away to a strange land. God saw Ruth's faithfulness, and he blessed her.

It's tempting to just do the easy thing sometimes—such as invite someone to church that you know will come. But it's the harder things—like inviting someone to church who might say no—that often have the greatest blessings.

HEROES KNOW THAT THE EASY WAY ISN'T ALWAYS THE BEST WAY.

Samuel Listens

Long before the Temple was built, the little boy Samuel lived in the Holy Tent with Eli the priest. Samuel served the priest, but God had another job for Samuel to do.

from 1 SAMUEL 3:1-19

The boy Samuel served the Lord under Eli. In those days the Lord did not speak directly to people very often. There were very few visions.

²Eli's eyes were so weak he was almost blind. One night he was lying in bed. ³Samuel was also in bed in the Lord's Holy Tent. The Box of the Agreement was in the Holy Tent. God's lamp was still burning.

⁴Then the Lord called Samuel. Samuel answered, "I am here!" ⁵He ran to Eli and said, "I am here. You called me."

But Eli said, "I didn't call you. Go back to bed." So Samuel went back to bed.

⁶The Lord called again, "Samuel!"

Samuel again went to Eli and said, "I am here. You called me."

Again Eli said, "I didn't call you. Go back to bed."

⁷Samuel did not yet know the Lord. The Lord had not spoken directly to him yet.

⁸The Lord called Samuel for the third time. Samuel got up and went to Eli. He said, "I am here. You called me."

Then Eli realized the Lord was calling the boy. ⁹So he told Samuel, "Go to bed. If he calls you again, say, 'Speak, Lord. I am your servant, and I am listening.'" So Samuel went and lay down in bed.

¹⁰The Lord came and stood there. He called as he had before. He said, "Samuel, Samuel!"

Samuel said, "Speak, Lord. I am your servant, and I am listening."

¹¹The Lord said to Samuel, "See, I am going to do something in Israel. It will shock those who hear about it. ¹²At that time I will do to Eli and his family everything I promised. I will not stop until I have finished. ¹³I told Eli I would punish his family forever. I will do it because Eli knew his sons were evil. They spoke against me, but he did not control them. ¹⁴So here is what I promised Eli's family: 'Your guilt will never be removed by sacrifice or offering.'"

¹⁵Samuel lay down until morning. Then he opened the doors of the Tent of the Lord. He was afraid to tell Eli about the vision. ¹⁶But Eli said to him, "Samuel, my son!"

Samuel answered, "I am here."

¹⁷Eli asked, "What did the Lord say to you? Don't hide it from me. May God punish you terribly if you hide from me anything he said to you." ¹⁸So Samuel told Eli everything. He did not hide anything from him. Then Eli said, "He is the Lord. Let him do what he thinks is best."

¹⁹The Lord was with Samuel as he grew up. He did not let any of Samuel's messages fail to come true.

When you pray, be like Samuel. Listen. Yes, God wants to hear all about your day, about the things you want and need, and about your hopes and fears. But God also wants you to "be quiet and know that I am God" (Psalm 46:10).

Chances are that you won't hear a big, booming voice from heaven; instead, a verse may pop into your mind, or a thought about someone who needs your prayers. God has a message for you, too, so take time listen to him—it's what heroes do.

HEROES TAKE TIME TO LISTEN TO GOD.

GOLIATH DARES
THE ISRAELITES
TO FIGHT HIM.

THE MIGHTY GOLIATH

> The Philistines had gathered for war against God's people. But what happened when a giant warrior met a boy with a giant faith?

from 1 SAMUEL 17:1-58

The Philistines gathered their armies for war. . . . ²Saul and the Israelites gathered in the Valley of Elah. And they camped there. They took their positions to fight the Philistines. ³The Philistines controlled one hill. The Israelites controlled another. The valley was between them.

⁴The Philistines had a champion fighter named Goliath. He was from Gath. He was about nine feet four inches tall.

He came out of the Philistine camp. [5]He had a bronze helmet on his head. And he wore a coat of scale armor. It was made of bronze and weighed about 125 pounds. [6]He wore bronze protectors on his legs. And he had a small spear of bronze tied on his back. [7]The wooden part of his larger spear was like a weaver's rod. And its blade weighed about 15 pounds. The officer who carried his shield walked in front of him.

[8]Goliath stood and shouted to the Israelite soldiers, "Why have you taken positions for battle? I am a Philistine, and you are Saul's servants! Choose a man and send him to fight me. [9]If he can fight and kill me, we will become your servants. But if I defeat and kill him, you will become our servants." [10]Then he said, "Today I stand and dare the army of Israel! Send one of your men to fight me!" [11]When Saul and the Israelites heard the Philistine's words, they were very afraid.

[12]Now David was the son of Jesse, an Ephrathite. Jesse was from Bethlehem in Judah. He had eight sons. In Saul's time Jesse was an old man. [13]His three oldest sons followed Saul to the war. The first son was Eliab. The second son was Abinadab. And the third son was Shammah. [14]David was the youngest son. Jesse's three oldest sons followed Saul. [15]But David went back and forth from Saul to Bethlehem. There he took care of his father's sheep.

[16]The Philistine Goliath came out every morning and evening. He stood before the Israelite army. This continued for 40 days.

[17]Now Jesse said to his son David, "Take this half bushel

of cooked grain. And take ten loaves of bread. Take them to your brothers in the camp. [18]Also take ten pieces of cheese. Give them to the commander of your brothers' group of 1,000 soldiers. See how your brothers are. Bring back something to show me they are all right. [19]Your brothers are with Saul and the army in the Valley of Elah. They are fighting against the Philistines."

[20]Early in the morning David left the sheep with another shepherd. He took the food and left as Jesse had told him. When David arrived at the camp, the army was leaving. They were going out to their battle positions. The soldiers were shouting their war cry. [21]The Israelites and Philistines were lining up their men to face each other in battle.

[22]David left the food with the man who kept the supplies. Then he ran to the battle line and talked to his brothers. [23]While he was talking with them, Goliath came out. He was the Philistine champion from Gath. He shouted things against Israel as usual, and David heard it. [24]When the Israelites saw Goliath, they were very much afraid and ran away.

[25]They said, "Look at this man Goliath. He keeps coming out to speak against Israel. The king will give much money to the man who kills Goliath. He will also give his daughter in marriage to whoever kills him. And his father's family will not have to pay taxes in Israel."

[26]David asked the men who stood near him, "What will be done to reward the man who kills this Philistine? What will be done for whoever takes away the shame from Israel? Goliath is a Philistine. He is not circumcised.

Why does he think he can speak against the armies of the living God?"

[27]The Israelites told David what they had been saying. They said, "This is what will be done for the man who kills Goliath."

[28]David's oldest brother Eliab heard David talking with the soldiers. He became angry with David. He asked David, "Why did you come here? Who's taking care of those few sheep of yours in the desert? I know you are proud. Your attitude is very bad. You came down here just to watch the battle!"

[29]David asked, "Now what have I done wrong? Can't I even talk?" [30]He then turned to other people and asked the same questions. And they gave him the same answer as before. [31]Some men heard what David said and told Saul. Then Saul ordered David to be sent to him.

[32]David said to Saul, "Don't let anyone be discouraged. I, your servant, will go and fight this Philistine!"

[33]Saul answered, "You can't go out against this Philistine and fight him. You're only a boy. Goliath has been a warrior since he was a young man."

[34]But David said to Saul, "I, your servant, have been keeping my father's sheep. When a lion or bear came and took a sheep from the flock, [35]I would chase it. I would attack it and save the sheep from its mouth. When it attacked me, I caught it by its fur. I would hit it and kill it. [36]I, your servant, have killed both a lion and a bear! Goliath, the Philistine who is not circumcised, will be like

the lion or bear I killed. He will die because he has stood against the armies of the living God. [37]The Lord saved me from a lion and a bear. He will also save me from this Philistine."

Saul said to David, "Go, and may the Lord be with you." [38]Saul put his own clothes on David. He put a bronze helmet on David's head and armor on his body. [39]David put on Saul's sword and tried to walk around. But he was not used to all the armor Saul had put on him.

He said to Saul, "I can't go in this. I'm not used to it." Then David took it all off. [40]He took his stick in his hand. And he chose five smooth stones from a stream. He put them in his pouch and held his sling in his hand. Then he went to meet Goliath.

[41]At the same time, the Philistine was coming closer to David. The man who held his shield walked in front of him. [42]Goliath looked at David. He saw that David was only a boy, tanned and handsome. He looked down at David with disgust. [43]He said, "Do you think I am a dog, that you come at me with a stick?" He used his gods' names to curse David. [44]He said to David, "Come here. I'll feed your body to the birds of the air and the wild animals!"

[45]But David said to him, "You come to me using a sword, a large spear and a small spear. But I come to you in the name of the Lord of heaven's armies. He's the God of the armies of Israel! You have spoken out against him. [46]Today the Lord will give you to me. I'll kill you, and I'll cut off your head. Today I'll feed the bodies of the Philistine

soldiers to the birds of the air and the wild animals. Then all the world will know there is a God in Israel! [47]Everyone gathered here will know the Lord does not need swords or spears to save people. The battle belongs to him! And he will help us defeat all of you."

[48]As Goliath came near to attack him, David ran quickly to meet him. [49]He took a stone from his pouch. He put it into his sling and slung it. The stone hit the Philistine on his forehead and sank into it. Goliath fell facedown on the ground.

[50]So David defeated the Philistine with only a sling and a stone! He hit him and killed him. He did not even have a sword in his hand. [51]David ran and stood beside the Philistine. He took Goliath's sword out of its holder and killed him. Then he cut off Goliath's head.

When the Philistines saw that their champion was dead, they turned and ran. [52]The men of Israel and Judah shouted and started chasing the Philistines. They chased them all the way to the entrance to the city of Gath. . . .

[53]The Israelites returned after chasing the Philistines. Then they took many things from the Philistine camp. [54]David took Goliath's head to Jerusalem. He also put Goliath's weapons in his own tent.

[55]Saul had watched David go out to meet Goliath. Saul spoke to Abner, commander of the army. He said, "Abner, who is that young man's father?"

Abner answered, "As surely as you live, my king, I do not know."

[56]The king said, "Find out whose son he is."

⁵⁷When David came back from killing Goliath, Abner brought him to Saul. David still held Goliath's head.

⁵⁸Saul asked him, "Young man, who is your father?"

David answered, "I am the son of your servant Jesse of Bethlehem."

Though Goliath was a mighty warrior and David was only a young shepherd, David stood up to him. David knew that God was on his side, and that made him undefeatable.

When you see something wrong, will you be brave enough to stop it? When that TV show uses God's name in a bad way, will you be brave enough to turn it off? When others say you're not allowed to pray, will you still pray? When you are laughed at for going to church, will you go anyway? When you stand up to do what is right, God promises that he will "make you strong and will help you" (Isaiah 41:10). God takes care of his heroes.

HEROES KNOW THAT GOD WILL GIVE THEM THE STRENGTH TO DO WHAT IS RIGHT.

WICKED KING AHAB AND QUEEN JEZEBEL REFUSE TO FOLLOW GOD'S LAWS.

JEZEBEL AND AHAB: A WICKED PAIR

King Ahab and Queen Jezebel were a perfect match—they were both perfectly evil! When they wanted something, they didn't care what it took or who they hurt to get it.

from 1 KINGS 21:1-25

A man named Naboth owned a vineyard. It was in Jezreel, near the palace of Ahab king of Israel. ²One day Ahab said to Naboth, "Give me your vineyard. It is near my palace. I want to make it into a vegetable garden. I will give you a better vineyard in its place. Or, if you prefer, I will pay you what it is worth."

³Naboth answered, "May the Lord keep me from ever giving my land to you. It belongs to my family."

⁴So Ahab went home, angry and upset. He did not like what Naboth from Jezreel had said. (Naboth had said, "I will not give you my family's land.") So Ahab lay down on his bed. He turned his face to the wall and refused to eat.

⁵His wife, Jezebel, came in. She asked him, "Why are you upset? Why do you refuse to eat?"

⁶Ahab answered, "I talked to Naboth, the man from Jezreel. I said, 'Sell me your vineyard. Or, if you prefer, I will give you another vineyard for it.' But Naboth refused."

⁷Jezebel answered, "Is this how you rule as king over Israel? Get out of bed. Eat something. Cheer up. I will get Naboth's vineyard for you."

⁸So Jezebel wrote some letters and signed Ahab's name to them. And she used his own seal to seal them. Then she sent them to the older leaders and important men who lived in Naboth's town. ⁹The letter she wrote said: "Declare a day during which the people are to give up eating. Call the people together. And give Naboth a place of honor among them. ¹⁰Seat two troublemakers across from him. Have them say they heard Naboth speak against God and the king. Then take Naboth out of the city and kill him with stones."

¹¹So the elders and important men of Jezreel obeyed Jezebel's command. ¹²They declared a special day. On that

day the people were to give up eating. They called the people together. And they put Naboth in a place of honor before the people. ¹³Then two troublemakers sat across from Naboth. They said they had heard Naboth speak against God and the king. So the people carried Naboth out of the city. And they killed him with stones. ¹⁴Then the leaders sent a message to Jezebel. It said, "Naboth has been killed."

¹⁵When Jezebel heard that Naboth had been killed, she told Ahab. She said, "Naboth of Jezreel is dead. Now you may go and take for yourself his vineyard you wanted." ¹⁶When Ahab heard that Naboth was dead, he left. He went to the vineyard to take it for his own.

¹⁷At this time the Lord spoke his word to Elijah. (Elijah was the prophet from Tishbe.) The Lord said, ¹⁸"Go to Ahab king of Israel, who rules in Samaria. He is at Naboth's vineyard to take it as his own. ¹⁹Tell Ahab that I, the Lord, say to him, 'Ahab! You have murdered Naboth and have taken his land. So I tell you this! In the same place that Naboth died, you will also die. The dogs that licked up Naboth's blood will lick up your blood in the same place!'"

²⁰When Ahab saw Elijah, he said, "So you have found me, my enemy!"

Elijah answered, "Yes, I have found you. You have always chosen to do what the Lord says is wrong. ²¹So the Lord says to you, 'I will destroy you. I will kill you and every male in your family, both slave and free. ²²Your family will be like the family of King Jeroboam son of Nebat. And it will be like the family of King Baasha son of Ahijah. Both of these families were completely destroyed. I will do this to you because you have made me angry. And you have caused the people of Israel to sin.'

²³"And the Lord also says, 'Dogs will eat the body of Jezebel in the city of Jezreel.'" . . .

²⁵There was no one like Ahab. No one had so often chosen to do what the Lord said was wrong. His wife Jezebel influenced him to do evil.

Ahab wanted Naboth's vineyard, and Jezebel wanted him to have it. She would do whatever it took to get it—even murder! And that didn't seem to bother Ahab in the least. Villains are like that.

Everyone wants things that they cannot have, and sometimes those things belong to someone else. But it's what you do with that "want" that matters. Will you lie, cheat, or steal to get that cool new phone, those shoes, or that candy bar? Or will you accept that sometimes the answer is no and just walk away?

HEROES DON'T ALWAYS GET WHAT THEY WANT . . . BUT THEY TRUST GOD FOR ALL THAT THEY NEED.

Mordecai
and the King

Mordecai was one of many Jews who had been
brought as captives to King Xerxes' land. Now, the
king's search for a new queen has taken his young
cousin Esther. So when Mordecai overheard a plot to
kill the king, what would he do?

from ESTHER 2:1-23

King Xerxes' . . . ²personal servants had a suggestion.
They said, "Let a search be made for beautiful young
virgins for the king. ³Let the king choose supervisors in

every area of his kingdom. Let them bring every beautiful young virgin to the palace at Susa. These women should be taken to the women's quarters and put under the care of Hegai. He is the king's eunuch in charge of the women. And let beauty treatments be given to them. ⁴Then let the girl who most pleases the king become queen in place of Vashti." The king liked this advice. So he did as they said.

⁵Now there was a Jewish man in the palace of Susa. His name was Mordecai. . . . ⁶Mordecai was part of the group taken into captivity with Jehoiachin king of Judah. ⁷Mordecai had a cousin named Hadassah, who had no father or mother. So Mordecai took care of her. Hadassah was also called Esther, and she had a very pretty figure and face. Mordecai had adopted her as his own daughter when her father and mother died.

⁸The king's command and order had been heard. And many girls had been brought to the palace in Susa. They had been put under the care of Hegai. When this happened, Esther was also taken to the king's palace. She was put into the care of Hegai, who was in charge of the women. ⁹Esther pleased Hegai, and he liked her. So Hegai quickly began giving Esther her beauty treatments and special food. . . .

¹⁰Esther did not tell anyone about her family or who her people were. Mordecai had told her not to. ¹¹Every day Mordecai walked back and forth near the courtyard. This was where the king's women lived. He wanted to find out how Esther was and what was happening to her.

¹²Before a girl could take her turn with King Xerxes,

she had to complete 12 months of beauty treatments. These were ordered for the women. For 6 months she was treated with oil and myrrh. And she spent 6 months with perfumes and cosmetics. [13]Then she was ready to go to the king. Anything she asked for was given to her. She could take it with her from the women's quarters to the king's palace. [14]In the evening she would go to the king's palace. And in the morning she would return to another part of the women's quarters. There she would be placed under the care of a man named Shaashgaz. Shaashgaz was the king's eunuch in charge of the slave women. The girl would not go back to the king again unless he was pleased with her. . . .

[15]Esther daughter of Abihail, Mordecai's uncle, had been adopted by Mordecai. The time came for Esther to go to the king. She asked for only what Hegai suggested she should take. . . . [16]So Esther was taken to King Xerxes in the royal palace. This happened in the tenth month, the month of Tebeth. It was in Xerxes' seventh year as king.

[17]And he liked her more than any of the others. So King Xerxes put a royal crown on Esther's head. And he made her queen in place of Vashti. . . .

[19]Now Mordecai was sitting at the king's gate. This was when the virgins were gathered the second time. [20]And Esther had still not told anyone about her family or who her people were. That is what Mordecai had told her to do. She still obeyed Mordecai just as she had done when he was bringing her up.

[21]Now Bigthana and Teresh were two of the king's officers who guarded the doorway. While Mordecai was sitting at the king's gate, Bigthana and Teresh became angry at the king. And they began to make plans to kill King Xerxes. [22]But Mordecai found out about their plans and told Queen Esther. Then Queen Esther told the king. She also told him that Mordecai had found out about the evil plan. [23]When the report was investigated, it was found to be true. The two officers who had planned to kill the king were hanged. And all this was written down in the daily court record in the king's presence.

Mordecai had good reasons not to like King Xerxes. He had been forced to come to this foreign land, King Xerxes did not worship God, and his young cousin, Esther, had even been forced to marry the king. So why would Mordecai help King Xerxes? Because it was the right thing to do.

God doesn't ask you to be kind only to those people who are good and kind to you. Instead, he asks you to "love your enemies. Pray for those who hurt you" (Matthew 5:44).

BEING A HERO ISN'T ALWAYS ABOUT BEING TOUGH; SOMETIMES IT'S ABOUT BEING KIND.

HAMAN THE TERRIBLE

Haman was a powerful man in King Xerxes' kingdom. He could have used that power to help others, but instead he used it to plot evil against God's people.

from **ESTHER 3:1-15**

King Xerxes honored Haman son of Hammedatha the Agagite. He gave Haman a new rank that was higher than all the important men. ²And all the royal officers at the king's gate would bow down and kneel before Haman. This was what the king had ordered. But Mordecai would not bow down, and he did not kneel. . . .

⁵Then Haman saw that Mordecai would not bow

down to him or kneel before him. And he became very angry. [6]He had been told who the people of Mordecai were. And he thought of himself as too important to try to kill only Mordecai. So he looked for a way to destroy all of Mordecai's people, the Jews, in all of Xerxes' kingdom. . . .

[8]Then Haman said to King Xerxes, "There is a certain group of people in all the areas of your kingdom. They are scattered among the other people. They keep themselves separate. Their customs are different from those of all the other people. And they do not obey the king's laws. It is not right for you to allow them to continue living in your kingdom. [9]If it pleases the king, let an order be given to destroy those people. Then I will pay 375 tons of silver to those who do the king's business. They will put it into the royal treasury."

[10]So the king took his signet ring off and gave it to Haman. Haman son of Hammedatha, the Agagite, was the enemy of the Jews. [11]Then the king said to Haman, "The money and the people are yours. Do with them as you please."

[12]On the thirteenth day of the first month, the royal secretaries were called. They wrote out all of Haman's orders. . . . They were written in the name of King Xerxes and sealed with his signet ring. [13]Letters were sent by messengers to all the king's empire. They stated the king's order to destroy, kill and completely wipe out all the Jews. That meant young and old, women and little children, too. The order said to kill all the Jews on a single day. That

was to be the thirteenth day of the twelfth month, which was Adar. And it said to take all the things that belonged to the Jews. [14]A copy of the order was to be given out as a law in every area. It was to be made known to all the people so that they would be ready for that day.

[15]The messengers set out, hurried by the king's command. At the same time the order was given in the palace at Susa. And the king and Haman sat down to drink.

> *Haman was full of pride and selfishness. He believed that he was better than everyone else. So when Mordecai refused to bow down to him, Haman was furious. He set out to destroy not only Mordecai, but all of God's people.*
>
> *God wants you to know that you are his own wonderful creation—just as each and every person is his own wonderful creation. No one is better than anyone else. Don't "let selfishness and pride be your guide. Be humble and give more honor to others than to yourselves" (Philippians 2:3).*

A REAL HERO ISN'T AFRAID TO HONOR OTHERS.

BRAVE QUEEN
ESTHER GOES
TO THE KING
TO SAVE HER
PEOPLE.

ESTHER MUST CHOOSE

No one in the palace knew that beautiful Queen Esther was a Jew. So when wicked Haman's plot put all the Jewish people in danger, would Esther choose to risk her own life to save her people?

from ESTHER 4:1–9:1

Now Mordecai heard about all that had been done. To show how upset he was, he tore his clothes. Then he put on rough cloth and ashes. And he went out into the city crying loudly and very sadly. [2]But Mordecai went only as far as the king's gate. This was because no one was allowed to enter that gate dressed in rough cloth. [3]The king's order reached every area. And there was great sadness and loud crying among the Jews. . . .

[4]Esther's servant girls and eunuchs came to her and told her about Mordecai. Esther was very upset and afraid. She sent clothes for Mordecai to put on instead of the rough cloth. But he would not wear them. [5]Then Esther called for Hathach. He was one of the king's eunuchs chosen by the king to serve her. Esther ordered him to find out what was bothering Mordecai and why.

[6]So Hathach went to Mordecai. Mordecai was in the city square in front of the king's gate. [7]Then Mordecai told Hathach everything that had happened to him. And he told Hathach about the amount of money Haman had promised to pay into the king's treasury for the killing of the Jews. [8]Mordecai also gave him a copy of the order to kill the Jews, which had been given in Susa. He wanted Hathach to show it to Esther and to tell her about it. And Mordecai told him to order Esther to go into the king's presence. He wanted her to beg for mercy and to plead with him for her people.

[9]Hathach went back and reported to Esther everything Mordecai had said. [10]Then Esther told Hathach to say to Mordecai, [11]"All the royal officers and people of the royal areas know this: No man or woman may go to the king in the inner courtyard without being called. There is only one law about this. Anyone who enters must be put to death. But

if the king holds out his gold scepter, that person may live. And I have not been called to go to the king for 30 days."

¹²And Esther's message was given to Mordecai. ¹³Then Mordecai gave orders to say to Esther: "Just because you live in the king's palace, don't think that out of all the Jews you alone will escape. ¹⁴You might keep quiet at this time. Then someone else will help and save the Jews. But you and your father's family will all die. And who knows, you may have been chosen queen for just such a time as this."

¹⁵Then Esther sent this answer to Mordecai: ¹⁶"Go and get all the Jews in Susa together. For my sake, give up eating. Do not eat or drink for three days, night and day. I and my servant girls will also give up eating. Then I will go to the king, even though it is against the law. And if I die, I die."

¹⁷So Mordecai went away. He did everything Esther had told him to do.

5 ¹On the third day Esther put on her royal robes. Then she stood in the inner courtyard of the king's palace, facing the king's hall. The king was sitting on his royal throne in the hall, facing the doorway. ²The king saw Queen Esther standing in the courtyard. When he saw her, he was very pleased. He held out to her the gold scepter that was in his hand. So Esther went up to him and touched the end of the scepter.

³Then the king asked, "What is it, Queen Esther? What do you want to ask me?" . . .

⁴Esther answered, "My king, if it pleases you, come today with Haman to a banquet. I have prepared it for him."

[5]Then the king said, "Bring Haman quickly so we may do what Esther asks."

So the king and Haman went to the banquet Esther had prepared for them. [6]As they were drinking wine, the king said to Esther, "Now, Esther, what are you asking for? I will give it to you. What is it you want? I will give you as much as half of my kingdom."

[7]Esther answered, . . . [8] "Come with Haman tomorrow to the banquet I will prepare for you. Then I will answer your question about what I want."

[9]Haman left the king's palace that day happy and content. Then he saw Mordecai at the king's gate. And he saw that Mordecai did not stand up nor did he tremble with fear before him. So Haman became very angry with Mordecai. [10]But he controlled his anger and went home.

Then Haman called his friends and Zeresh, his wife, together. . . . [11]And he told them how the king had placed him higher than his important men and his royal officers. [12]"And that's not all," Haman added. "I'm the only person Queen Esther invited to come with the king to the banquet she gave. And tomorrow also the queen has asked me to be her guest with the king. [13]But all this does not really make me happy. I'm not happy as long as I see that Jew Mordecai sitting at the king's gate."

[14]Then Haman's wife Zeresh and all his friends said, "Have a platform built to hang someone. Build it 75 feet high. And in the morning ask the king to have Mordecai hanged on it. Then go to the banquet with the king and

be happy." Haman liked this suggestion. So he ordered the platform to be built. . . .

7 ¹So the king and Haman went in to eat with Queen Esther. ²They were drinking wine. And the king said to Esther on this second day also, "What are you asking for? I will give it to you. What is it you want? I will give you as much as half of my kingdom."

³Then Queen Esther answered, "My king, I hope you are pleased with me. If it pleases you, let me live. This is what I ask. And let my people live, too. This is what I want. ⁴I ask this because my people and I have been sold to be destroyed. We are to be killed and completely wiped out. . . ."

⁵Then King Xerxes asked Queen Esther, "Who is he? Where is he? Who has done such a thing?"

⁶Esther said, "A man who is against us! Our enemy is this wicked Haman!"

Then Haman was filled with terror before the king and queen. ⁷The king was very angry. He got up, left his wine and went out into the palace garden. But Haman stayed inside to beg Queen Esther to save his life. He could see that the king had already decided to kill him.

⁸The king came back from the palace garden to the banquet hall. And he saw Haman falling on the couch

where Esther was lying. The king said, "Will he even attack the queen while I am in the house?"

As soon as the king said that, servants came in and covered Haman's face. [9]Harbona was one of the eunuchs there serving the king. He said, "Look, a platform for hanging people stands near Haman's house. It is 75 feet high. This is the one Haman had prepared for Mordecai, who gave the warning that saved the king."

The king said, "Hang Haman on it!" [10]So they hanged Haman on the platform he had prepared for Mordecai. Then the king was not so angry anymore. . . .

8[3]Once again Esther spoke to the king. She fell at the king's feet and cried. . . . [5]She said, "My king, I hope you are pleased with me. And maybe it will please you to do this. You might think it is the right thing to do. And maybe you are happy with me. If so, let an order be written to cancel the letters Haman wrote. [6]I could not stand to see that terrible thing happen to my people." . . .

[7]King Xerxes answered Queen Esther and Mordecai the Jew. He said, "Because Haman was against the Jews, I have given his things to Esther. And my soldiers have hanged him. [8]Now write another order in the king's name. Write it to the Jews as it seems best to you. Then seal the order with the king's signet ring. . . .

¹¹These were the king's orders: The Jews in every city have the right to gather together to protect themselves. They have the right to destroy, kill and completely wipe out the army of any area or people who attack them. . . .

9¹The order the king had commanded was to be done on the thirteenth day of the twelfth month. . . . So the Jews themselves defeated those who hated them.

Esther had a choice to make. God had given her a chance to save her people, but it meant going to the king uninvited, which was dangerous—he could have her killed on the spot! So Esther first went to God, asking for his help. Only then did she go to the king. God saved Esther and all the Jewish people.

God has a plan for you and your life. Sometimes God's plans are easy and even fun. But sometimes they are hard. When God asks you to do something hard, remember Esther, and go to God first!

HEROES KNOW THAT THE GREATEST ADVENTURES BEGIN ON THEIR KNEES . . . IN PRAYER!

GOD KEEPS DANIEL SAFE IN THE LIONS' DEN.

DANIEL PRAYS

> Daniel was an important man in King Darius' kingdom, but even Daniel had to obey the law. So when the law of the land went against the law of the Lord, what would Daniel do?

from DANIEL 5:31-6:27

A man named Darius the Mede became the new king. Darius was 62 years old.

6 ¹Darius thought it would be a good idea to choose 120 governors. They would rule through all of his kingdom. ²And he chose three men as supervisors over those 120 governors. Daniel was one of these three supervisors. The king set up these men so that he would not be cheated. ³Daniel showed that he could do the work better than the other supervisors and the governors. Because of this, the king planned to put Daniel in charge of the whole kingdom. ⁴So the other supervisors and the governors tried to find reasons to accuse Daniel. But he went on doing the business of the government. And they could not find anything wrong with him. So they could not accuse him of doing anything wrong. Daniel was trustworthy. He was not lazy and did not cheat the king. ⁵Finally these men said, "We will never find any reason to accuse Daniel. But we must find something to complain about. It will have to be about the law of his God."

⁶So the supervisors and the governors went as a group to the king. They said: "King Darius, live forever! ⁷The supervisors, assistant governors, governors, the people who advise you and the captains of the soldiers have all agreed on something. We think the king should make this law that everyone would have to obey: No one should pray to any god or man except to you, our king. This should be done for the next 30 days. Anyone who doesn't obey will be thrown into the lions' den. ⁸Now, our king, make the law. Write it down so it cannot be changed. The laws of the Medes and Persians cannot be canceled." ⁹So King Darius made the law and had it written.

[10]When Daniel heard that the new law had been written, he went to his house. He went to his upstairs room. The windows of that room opened toward Jerusalem. Three times each day Daniel got down on his knees and prayed. He prayed and thanked God, just as he always had done.

[11]Then those men went as a group and found Daniel. They saw him praying and asking God for help. [12]So they went to the king. They talked to him about the law he had made. They said, "Didn't you write a law that says no one may pray to any god or man except you, our king? Doesn't it say that anyone who disobeys during the next 30 days will be thrown into the lions' den?"

The king answered, "Yes, I wrote that law. And the laws of the Medes and Persians cannot be canceled."

[13]Then those men spoke to the king. They said, "Daniel is one of the captives from Judah. And he is not paying attention to the law you wrote. Daniel still prays to his God three times every day." [14]The king became very upset when he heard this. He decided he had to save Daniel. He worked until sunset trying to think of a way to save him.

[15]Then those men went as a group to the king. They said, "Remember, our king, the law of the Medes and Persians. It says that no law or command given by the king can be changed."

[16]So King Darius gave the order. They brought Daniel and threw him into the lions' den. The king said to Daniel, "May the God you serve all the time save you!" [17]A big stone was brought. It was put over the opening of the lions'

den. Then the king used his signet ring to put his special seal on the rock. And he used the rings of his royal officers to put their seals on the rock also. This showed that no one could move that rock and bring Daniel out. [18]Then King Darius went back to his palace. He did not eat that night. He did not have any entertainment brought to entertain him. And he could not sleep.

[19]The next morning King Darius got up at dawn. He hurried to the lions' den. [20]As he came near the den, he was worried. He called out to Daniel. He said, "Daniel, servant of the living God! Has your God that you always worship been able to save you from the lions?"

[21]Daniel answered, "My king, live forever! [22]My God sent his angel to close the lions' mouths. They have not hurt me, because my God knows I am innocent. I never did anything wrong to you, my king."

[23]King Darius was very happy. He told his servants to lift Daniel out of the lions' den. So they lifted him out and did not find any injury on him. This was because Daniel had trusted in his God.

[24]Then the king gave a command. The men who had accused Daniel were brought to the lions' den and thrown into it. Their wives and children were also thrown into it. The lions grabbed them before they hit the floor of the den. And the lions crushed their bones.

[25]Then King Darius wrote a letter. It was to all people and all nations, to those who spoke every language in the world:

I wish you great wealth.

[26]I am making a new law. This law is for people in every part of my kingdom. All of you must fear and respect the God of Daniel. Daniel's God is the living God. He lives forever. His kingdom will never be destroyed. His rule will never end. [27]God rescues and saves people. God does mighty miracles in heaven and on earth. God saved Daniel from the power of the lions.

Daniel only wanted to pray to God, but now that was against the law. Daniel could have stormed into the palace and yelled at the king. He could have fought the men who came to arrest him. But instead, Daniel did what he knew the Lord wanted him to do.

When you decide to follow Jesus, you sometimes have to make tough choices. You won't be thrown to the lions these days, but you might be made fun of or left out. So do you go along with your friends when they see a movie that you know Jesus wouldn't want you to see? Do you listen to those songs that Jesus wouldn't sing? You don't have to yell or throw a fit. Just do what you know Jesus would want you to do.

HEROES DO WHAT THEY KNOW GOD WANTS THEM TO DO.

JONAH IS
ABOUT TO
MEET A VERY
BIG FISH!

Jonah: A Hero Gets A Second Chance

Nobody liked Nineveh. The people there did all sorts of evil. They deserved to be destroyed—at least that's what Jonah the prophet thought. Was he right?

from JONAH 1:1-3:10

The Lord spoke his word to Jonah son of Amittai: ²"Get up, go to the great city of Nineveh and preach against it. I see the evil things they do."

³But Jonah got up to run away from the Lord. He went to the city of Joppa. There he found a ship that was going to the city of Tarshish. Jonah paid for the trip and went aboard. He wanted to go to Tarshish to run away from the Lord.

⁴But the Lord sent a great wind on the sea. This wind made the sea very rough. So the ship was in danger of breaking apart. ⁵The sailors were afraid. Each man cried to his own god. The men began throwing the cargo into the sea. This would make the ship lighter so it would not sink.

But Jonah had gone down into the ship to lie down. He fell fast asleep. ⁶The captain of the ship came and said, "Why are you sleeping? Get up! Pray to your god! Maybe your god will pay attention to us. Maybe he will save us!"

⁷Then the men said to each other, "Let's throw lots to see who caused these troubles to happen to us."

So the men threw lots. The lot showed that the trouble had happened because of Jonah. . . . ¹⁰Then the men were very afraid. They asked Jonah, "What terrible thing did you do?" They knew Jonah was running away from the Lord because Jonah had told them. . . .

¹¹"What should we do to you to make the sea calm down?"

¹²Jonah said to them, "Pick me up, and throw me into the sea. Then it will calm down. I know it is my fault that this great storm has come on you."

¹³Instead, the men tried to row the ship back to the

land. But they could not. The wind and the waves of the sea were becoming much stronger.

¹⁴So the men cried to the Lord, "Lord, please don't let us die because of taking this man's life. Please don't think we are guilty of killing an innocent man. Lord, you have caused all this to happen. You wanted it this way." ¹⁵Then the men picked up Jonah and threw him into the sea. So the sea became calm. ¹⁶Then they began to fear the Lord very much. They offered a sacrifice to the Lord. They also made promises to him.

¹⁷And the Lord caused a very big fish to swallow Jonah. Jonah was in the stomach of the fish three days and three nights.

2 ¹While Jonah was in the stomach of the fish, he prayed to the Lord his God. . . . Jonah said,

> ² *"I was in danger.*
> *So I called to the Lord, and he answered me.*
> *I was about to die.*
> *So I cried to you, and you heard my voice.*
> ³ *You threw me into the sea.*
> *I went down, down into the deep sea.*
> *The water was all around me.*
> *Your powerful waves flowed over me.*
> ⁴ *I said, 'I was driven out of your presence.*
> *But I hope to see your Holy Temple again.'*
> ⁵ *The waters of the sea closed over me.*
> *I was about to die.*
> *The deep sea was all around me.*

> Seaweed wrapped around my head.
> ⁶I went down to where the mountains of the sea
>   start to rise.
>   I thought I was locked in this prison forever.
> But you saved me from death, Lord my God.
> ⁷"When my life had almost gone,
>   I remembered the Lord.
> Lord, I prayed to you.
>   And you heard my prayers. . . ."

¹⁰Then the Lord spoke to the fish. And the fish spit Jonah out of its stomach onto the dry land.

3 ¹Then the Lord spoke his word to Jonah again. The Lord said, ²"Get up. Go to the great city Nineveh. Preach against it what I tell you."

³So Jonah obeyed the Lord. He got up and went to Nineveh. It was a very large city. It took a person three days just to walk across it. ⁴Jonah entered the city. When he had walked for one day, he preached to the people. He said, "After 40 days, Nineveh will be destroyed!"

⁵The people of Nineveh believed in God. They announced they would stop eating for a while. They put on rough cloth to show how sad they were. . . . ⁶When the king of Nineveh heard this news, he got up from his throne. He took off his robe. He covered himself with rough cloth and sat in ashes to show how upset he was.

⁷He made an announcement and sent it through the city. The announcement said:

By command of the king and his important men: No person or animal should eat anything. No herd or flock will be allowed to taste anything. Do not let them eat food or drink water. ⁸But every person and animal should be covered with rough cloth. People should cry loudly to God. Everyone must turn away from his evil life. Everyone must stop doing harm. ⁹Maybe God will change his mind. Maybe he will stop being angry. Then we will not die.

¹⁰God saw what the people did. He saw that they stopped doing evil things. So God changed his mind and did not do what he had warned. He did not punish them.

Jonah had already decided that the people of Nineveh were so evil that they deserved to be destroyed, not forgiven. But God wanted to give the people of Nineveh a second chance. So God gave Jonah a second chance to obey him.

Everyone makes mistakes—even heroes. But when you see someone doing wrong, it's not up to you to punish him. God hopes that you will "help those who are weak," and "try to do what is good for each other" (1 Thessalonians 5:14–15). That's what heroes do.

HEROES GIVE . . . AND GET . . . SECOND CHANCES.

THE
NEW
TESTAMENT

THE ANGEL
GABRIEL TELLS
MARY OF THE
COMING OF BABY
JESUS.

Mary and the Angel

Mary was a young girl, engaged to be married. She had her life all planned out. But what did she do when an angel appeared with a message from God that would change everything?

from LUKE 1:26-45

God sent the angel Gabriel to a virgin who lived in Nazareth, a town in Galilee. She was engaged to marry a man named Joseph from the family of David.

Her name was Mary. [28]The angel came to her and said, "Greetings! The Lord has blessed you and is with you."

[29]But Mary was very confused by what the angel said. Mary wondered, "What does this mean?"

[30]The angel said to her, "Don't be afraid, Mary, because God is pleased with you. [31]Listen! You will become pregnant. You will give birth to a son, and you will name him Jesus. [32]He will be great, and people will call him the Son of the Most High. The Lord God will give him the throne of King David, his ancestor. [33]He will rule over the people of Jacob forever. His kingdom will never end."

[34]Mary said to the angel, "How will this happen? I am a virgin!"

[35]The angel said to Mary, "The Holy Spirit will come upon you, and the power of the Most High will cover you. The baby will be holy. He will be called the Son of God. [36]Now listen! Elizabeth, your relative, is very old. But she is also pregnant with a son. Everyone thought she could not have a baby, but she has been pregnant for six months. [37]God can do everything!"

[38]Mary said, "I am the servant girl of the Lord. Let this happen to me as you say!" Then the angel went away.

[39]Mary got up and went quickly to a town in the mountains of Judea. [40]She went to Zechariah's house and greeted Elizabeth. [41]When Elizabeth heard Mary's greeting, the unborn baby inside Elizabeth jumped. Then Elizabeth was filled with the Holy Spirit. [42]She cried out in a loud voice, "God has blessed you more than any other woman.

And God has blessed the baby which you will give birth to. ⁴³You are the mother of my Lord, and you have come to me! Why has something so good happened to me? ⁴⁴When I heard your voice, the baby inside me jumped with joy. ⁴⁵You are blessed because you believed what the Lord said to you would really happen."

God's plan for Mary was going to change everything. People would make fun of her and avoid her. And what would Joseph do? Would he still marry her? Life was going to be much more difficult. Mary could have said no. But she didn't.

Are you willing to be embarrassed for God? Are you ready to pray over your food in public, even when no one else does? Are you willing to go to church when all your friends are going to the ballgame? The Bible promises that "when people insult you because you follow Christ, then you are blessed." (1 Peter 4:14).

HEROES KNOW THAT SERVING GOD ISN'T ALWAYS EASY, BUT IT'S ALWAYS WORTH IT!

JOSEPH OBEYS QUICKLY

Joseph had a plan for his future. He thought he knew exactly what should happen. He would marry Mary, and they would have children and grow old together. Just an ordinary family. But God had a different plan—a very different plan. Would Joseph choose to follow God's way or his own?

from MATTHEW 1:18-25

The mother of Jesus Christ was Mary. And this is how the birth of Jesus came about. Mary was engaged to marry Joseph. But before they married, she learned that she was going to have a baby. She was pregnant by the power of the Holy Spirit. [19]Mary's husband, Joseph, was a good man. He did not want to disgrace her in public, so he planned to divorce her secretly.

[20]While Joseph thought about this, an angel of the Lord came to him in a dream. The angel said, "Joseph, descendant of David, don't be afraid to take Mary as your wife. The baby in her is from the Holy Spirit. [21]She will give birth to a son. You will name the son Jesus. Give him that name because he will save his people from their sins."

[22]All this happened to make clear the full meaning of what the Lord had said through the prophet: [23]"The virgin will be pregnant. She will have a son, and they will name him Immanuel." This name means "God is with us."

[24]When Joseph woke up, he did what the Lord's angel had told him to do. Joseph married Mary. [25]But he did not have sexual relations with her until she gave birth to the son. And Joseph named the son Jesus.

All Joseph's plans were falling apart, and he believed he must abandon Mary. But then an angel appeared and everything changed again. The angel told him that the baby was the Son of God, and that he must take Mary as his wife. And that's just what Joseph did. Not a few days or weeks later. But right away, "when Joseph woke up."

It's easy to say, "Okay, I'll . . . pick up my room . . . say my prayers . . . invite someone to church." But saying it isn't enough; you have to actually do it. Not in a few hours or a few days, but right away. Psalm 119:60 says, "I hurried and did not wait to obey your commands"—now, that's a hero in action.

GOD LOVES A HERO WHO QUICKLY OBEYS.

The Shepherds Can't Wait

God's own Son left the wonders of heaven and came to earth. Whom did he choose to appear to first?

from LUKE 2:1-21

At that time, Augustus Caesar sent an order to all people in the countries that were under Roman rule. The order said that they must list their names in a register. ²This was the first registration taken while Quirinius was governor of Syria. ³And everyone went to their own towns to be registered.

⁴So Joseph left Nazareth, a town in Galilee. He went to the

town of Bethlehem in Judea. This town was known as the town of David. Joseph went there because he was from the family of David. ⁵Joseph registered with Mary because she was engaged to marry him. (Mary was now pregnant.) ⁶While Joseph and Mary were in Bethlehem, the time came for her to have the baby. ⁷She gave birth to her first son. There were no rooms left in the inn. So she wrapped the baby with cloths and laid him in a box where animals are fed.

⁸That night, some shepherds were in the fields nearby watching their sheep. ⁹An angel of the Lord stood before them. The glory of the Lord was shining around them, and suddenly they became very frightened. ¹⁰The angel said to them, "Don't be afraid, because I am bringing you some good news. It will be a joy to all the people. ¹¹Today your Savior was born in David's town. He is Christ, the Lord. ¹²This is how you will know him: You will find a baby wrapped in cloths and lying in a feeding box."

¹³Then a very large group of angels from heaven joined the first angel. All the angels were praising God, saying:

¹⁴*"Give glory to God in heaven,*
and on earth let there be peace to the people
who please God."

¹⁵Then the angels left the shepherds and went back to heaven. The shepherds said to each other, "Let us go to Bethlehem and see this thing that has happened. We will see this thing the Lord told us about."

16So the shepherds went quickly and found Mary and Joseph. 17And the shepherds saw the baby lying in a feeding box. Then they told what the angels had said about this child. 18Everyone was amazed when they heard what the shepherds said to them. 19Mary hid these things in her heart; she continued to think about them. 20Then the shepherds went back to their sheep, praising God and thanking him for everything that they had seen and heard. It was just as the angel had told them.

21When the baby was eight days old, he was circumcised, and he was named Jesus. This name had been given by the angel before the baby began to grow inside Mary.

The shepherds were busy watching over their sheep. It was their job. But when the angels appeared praising God and telling about the birth of the Savior, they dropped everything and rushed off to see Jesus. No questions asked.

You have a chance to see Jesus too—in his Word and in his worship. Do you set aside a time each day to rush off to meet Jesus? To pray, to sing, to praise him? He's waiting for you.

HEROES CAN'T WAIT TO MEET JESUS IN HIS WORD.

HEROD
TRIES TO
TRICK THE
WISE MEN.

HEROD'S GREED

Herod was king of Jerusalem, and he wanted to stay the king of Jerusalem—no matter what the cost!

from MATTHEW 2:1-18

Jesus was born in the town of Bethlehem in Judea during the time when Herod was king. After Jesus was born, some wise men from the east came to Jerusalem. ²They asked, "Where is the baby who was born to be the king of the Jews? We saw his star in the east. We came to worship him."

³When King Herod heard about this new king of the Jews, he was troubled. And all the people in Jerusalem were worried too. ⁴Herod called a meeting of all the leading priests and teachers of the law. He asked them where the Christ

would be born. ⁵They answered, "In the town of Bethlehem in Judea. The prophet wrote about this in the Scriptures:

⁶'*But you, Bethlehem, in the land of Judah,*
  you are important among the rulers of Judah.
A ruler will come from you.
  He will be like a shepherd for my people, the
  Israelites.'"

Micah 5:2

⁷Then Herod had a secret meeting with the wise men from the east. He learned from them the exact time they first saw the star. ⁸Then Herod sent the wise men to Bethlehem. He said to them, "Go and look carefully to find the child. When you find him, come tell me. Then I can go worship him too."

⁹The wise men heard the king and then left. They saw the same star they had seen in the east. It went before them until it stopped above the place where the child was. ¹⁰When the wise men saw the star, they were filled with joy. ¹¹They went to the house where the child was and saw him with his mother, Mary. They bowed down and worshiped the child. They opened the gifts they brought for him. They gave him treasures of gold, frankincense, and myrrh. ¹²But God warned the wise men in a dream not to go back to Herod. So they went home to their own country by a different way.

¹³After they left, an angel of the Lord came to Joseph in a dream. The angel said, "Get up! Take the child and his mother and escape to Egypt. Herod will start looking for

the child to kill him. Stay in Egypt until I tell you to return."

¹⁴So Joseph got up and left for Egypt during the night with the child and his mother. ¹⁵Joseph stayed in Egypt until Herod died. . . .

¹⁶When Herod saw that the wise men had tricked him, he was very angry. So he gave an order to kill all the baby boys in Bethlehem and in all the area around Bethlehem who were two years old or younger. This was in keeping with the time he learned from the wise men. ¹⁷So what God had said through the prophet Jeremiah came true: . . .

> ¹⁸*Rachel cries for her children,*
> *and she cannot be comforted,*
> *because her children are dead."*
> *Jeremiah 31:15*

Herod was greedy and selfish. He wanted the power of being king to be his and his alone. And he did terrible things to keep it all to himself.

Most terrible things start with greed and selfishness. But "God loves the person who gives happily" (2 Corinthians 9:7). Letting someone else go first, saving the bigger cookie for your brother or sister—that's what God's heroes do!

HEROES THINK OF OTHERS FIRST.

John the Baptist

John the Baptist had been miraculously born to Elizabeth and Zechariah in their old age. He was born to be God's messenger. God wanted John to tell the people that Jesus was coming.

from MATTHEW 3:1-17

About that time John the Baptist came and began preaching in the desert area of Judea. [2]John said, "Change your hearts and lives because the kingdom of heaven is coming soon." [3]John the Baptist is the one Isaiah the prophet was talking about. Isaiah said:

*"This is a voice of a man
who calls out in the desert:
'Prepare the way for the Lord. . . .'"*
Isaiah 40:3

⁴John's clothes were made from camel's hair. He wore a leather belt around his waist. For food, he ate locusts and wild honey. ⁵Many people went to hear John preach. They came from Jerusalem and all Judea and all the area around the Jordan River. ⁶They told of the sins they had done, and John baptized them in the Jordan River.

⁷Many of the Pharisees and Sadducees came to the place where John was baptizing people. When John saw them, he said: "You are snakes! Who warned you to run away from God's anger that is coming? ⁸You must do the things that show that you have really changed your hearts and lives. ⁹And don't think that you can say to yourselves, 'Abraham is our father.' I tell you that God could make children for Abraham from these rocks. ¹⁰The ax is now ready to cut down the trees. Every tree that does not produce good fruit will be cut down and thrown into the fire.

¹¹"I baptize you with water to show that your hearts and lives have changed. But there is one coming later who is greater than I am. I am not good enough to carry his sandals. He will baptize you with the Holy Spirit and with fire. ¹²He will come ready to clean the grain. He will separate the good grain from the chaff. He will put the good part of

the grain into his barn. And he will burn the chaff with a fire that cannot be put out."

¹³At that time Jesus came from Galilee to the Jordan River. He came to John and wanted John to baptize him. ¹⁴But John tried to stop him. John said, "Why do you come to me to be baptized? I should be baptized by you!"

¹⁵Jesus answered, "Let it be this way for now. We should do all things that are right." So John agreed to baptize Jesus.

¹⁶Jesus was baptized and came up out of the water. Heaven opened, and he saw God's Spirit coming down on him like a dove. ¹⁷And a voice spoke from heaven. The voice said, "This is my Son and I love him. I am very pleased with him."

John had to tell people about God's love and the coming of Jesus. It was too wonderful of a thing to keep to himself. Even when the Pharisees and Sadducees—who were the religious rulers of that time—became angry with him, John just couldn't stop preaching.

You have wonderful news to tell too. Even more wonderful than John's news. John didn't know the whole story of Jesus, but you do! Think about all the people that you could tell about Jesus—and then go tell them.

HEROES SHARE THE GOOD NEWS ABOUT JESUS WITH OTHERS.

SATAN, THE TEMPTER

Satan is the most evil villain in all of creation. He tempted the very first man and woman, and then he even came to tempt Jesus!

from MATTHEW 4:1-11

Then the Spirit led Jesus into the desert to be tempted by the devil. ²Jesus ate nothing for 40 days and nights. After this, he was very hungry. ³The devil came to Jesus to tempt him. The devil said, "If you are the Son of God, tell these rocks to become bread."

⁴Jesus answered, "It is written in the Scriptures, 'A person does not live only by eating bread. But a person lives by everything the Lord says.'"

[5]Then the devil led Jesus to the holy city of Jerusalem. He put Jesus on a very high place of the Temple. [6]The devil said, "If you are the Son of God, jump off. It is written in the Scriptures,

> 'He has put his angels in charge of you.
>   They will catch you with their hands.
>   And you will not hit your foot on a rock.'"
>   Psalm 91:11–12

[7]Jesus answered him, "It also says in the Scriptures, 'Do not test the Lord your God.'"

[8]Then the devil led Jesus to the top of a very high mountain. He showed Jesus all the kingdoms of the world and all the great things that are in those kingdoms. [9]The devil said, "If you will bow down and worship me, I will give you all these things."

[10]Jesus said to the devil, "Go away from me, Satan! It is written in the Scriptures, 'You must worship the Lord your God. Serve only him!'"

[11]So the devil left Jesus. And then some angels came to Jesus and helped him.

Satan tried to make Jesus sin. He tempted him with bread when Jesus was hungry. He tempted him with wealth and power. But to all of that Jesus said, "Go away from me, Satan!" (Matthew 4:10). When Jesus spoke God's Word to him, Satan left.

Satan will try to tempt you too. He'll tempt you to lie to get out of trouble. He'll tempt you to gossip about your friends. He'll tempt you in many different ways. But when you feel him tempting you to do the wrong thing, do just what Jesus did. Say, "Go away from me, Satan!" And then go to God's Word and remember that "when you are tempted, God will also give you a way to escape that temptation" (1 Corinthians 10:13).

HEROES OF FAITH TELL SATAN TO GO AWAY!

FOUR MEN LOWER THEIR PARALYZED FRIEND THROUGH THE ROOF TO JESUS.

Four Good Friends

Jesus healed people wherever he went. So, four men set out to take their paralyzed friend to Jesus to be healed. But the crowd was so thick, they couldn't get to Jesus. Would they find a way to help their friend?

from **MARK 2:1-12**

Jesus came back to Capernaum. The news spread that he was home. ²So many people gathered to hear him preach that the house was full. There was no place to stand, not even outside the door. Jesus was teaching them. ³Some people came, bringing a paralyzed man to Jesus. Four of them were carrying the paralyzed man. ⁴But they could not get to Jesus because of the crowd. So they went to the roof above Jesus and made a hole in the roof. Then they lowered the mat with the paralyzed man on it. ⁵Jesus saw that these men had great faith. So he said to the paralyzed man, "Young man, your sins are forgiven."

⁶Some of the teachers of the law were sitting there. They saw what Jesus did, and they said to themselves, ⁷"Why does this man say things like that? He is saying things that are against God. Only God can forgive sins."

⁸At once Jesus knew what these teachers of the law were thinking. So he said to them, "Why are you thinking these things? ⁹Which is easier: to tell this paralyzed man, 'Your sins are forgiven,' or to tell him, 'Stand up. Take your mat and walk'? ¹⁰But I will prove to you that the Son of Man has authority on earth to forgive sins." So Jesus said to the paralyzed man, ¹¹"I tell you, stand up. Take your mat and go home." ¹²Immediately the paralyzed man stood up. He took his mat and walked out while everyone was watching him.

The people were amazed and praised God. They said, "We have never seen anything like this!"

Four men wanted to help their friend. They carried him on his mat all the way to where Jesus was. But the house was so crowded, they could not get to Jesus. They could have simply given up and gone home. But instead they carried their friend up to the roof and dug through layers of dried plaster and reeds to lower their friend down to Jesus. They were true friends—and true heroes.

Sometimes being a true friend is easy, like when you're playing and having fun. But when your friend is being picked on, or is sick, or is just having a bad day and taking it out on you—that's when it can be hard to be a friend. But God says in Proverbs 17:17, "A friend loves you all the time"—even when it's tough. It's just what heroes do.

HEROES STICK BY THEIR FRIENDS . . . IN GOOD TIMES AND BAD!

JESUS USES A SMALL BOY'S LUNCH TO FEED THOUSANDS.

A Boy's Lunch

Thousands of people had gathered to listen to Jesus. But as the day went on, the people became hungry and tired. There was no place to get food. One little boy carried a small lunch, but was he willing to share? And how could one lunch possibly feed the thousands of people?

from JOHN 6:1-15

After this, Jesus went across Lake Galilee (or, Lake Tiberias). ²Many people followed him because they saw the miracles he did to heal the sick. ³Jesus went up on a hill and there sat down with his followers. ⁴It was almost the time for the Jewish Passover Feast.

⁵Jesus looked up and saw a large crowd coming toward him. He said to Philip, "Where can we buy bread for all these people to eat?" ⁶(Jesus asked Philip this question to test him. Jesus already knew what he planned to do.)

⁷Philip answered, "We would all have to work a month to buy enough bread for each person here to have only a little piece."

⁸Another follower there was Andrew. He was Simon Peter's brother. Andrew said, ⁹"Here is a boy with five loaves of barley bread and two little fish. But that is not enough for so many people."

¹⁰Jesus said, "Tell the people to sit down." This was a very grassy place. There were about 5,000 men who sat down there. ¹¹Then Jesus took the loaves of bread. He thanked God for the bread and gave it to the people who were sitting there. He did the same with the fish. He gave them as much as they wanted.

¹²They all had enough to eat. When they had finished, Jesus said to his followers, "Gather the pieces of fish and bread that were not eaten. Don't waste anything." ¹³So they gathered up the pieces that were left. They filled 12 large baskets with the pieces that were left of the five barley loaves.

¹⁴The people saw this miracle that Jesus did. They said, "He must truly be the Prophet who is coming into the world."

¹⁵Jesus knew that the people planned to come and take him by force and make him their king. So he left and went into the hills alone.

The boy didn't think he had very much; it was just his lunch. A couple of fish and five small loaves of bread. But he gave it to Jesus, and Jesus made it more than enough. Jesus made him a hero of faith.

You may think that you don't have very much to give Jesus. Just a little time, or work, or a few coins. But if you—even as a child—give what you can, with all your heart, Jesus will make it more than enough. He promises, "Give, and you will receive. . . . It will be poured into your hands—more than you can hold" (Luke 6:38).

HEROES HAPPILY GIVE TO GOD.

A SAMARITAN STOPS TO HELP A JEWISH MAN.

A SAMARITAN'S CHOICE

The Samaritan people and the Jewish people hated each other, and they never helped each other. So when a Samaritan stumbled across a Jewish man lying hurt in the road, would he just keep on walking?

from LUKE 10:25-37

Then a teacher of the law stood up. He was trying to test Jesus. He said, "Teacher, what must I do to get life forever?"

²⁶Jesus said to him, "What is written in the law? What do you read there?"

²⁷The man answered, "Love the Lord your God. Love him with all your heart, all your soul, all your strength, and all your mind." Also, "You must love your neighbor as you love yourself."

²⁸Jesus said to him, "Your answer is right. Do this and you will have life forever."

²⁹But the man wanted to show that the way he was living was right. So he said to Jesus, "And who is my neighbor?"

³⁰To answer this question, Jesus said, "A man was going down the road from Jerusalem to Jericho. Some robbers attacked him. They tore off his clothes and beat him. Then they left him lying there, almost dead. ³¹It happened that a Jewish priest was going down that road. When the priest saw the man, he walked by on the other side of the road. ³²Next, a Levite came there. He went over and looked at the man. Then he walked by on the other side of the road. ³³Then a Samaritan traveling down the road came to where the hurt man was lying. He saw the man and felt very sorry for him. ³⁴The Samaritan went to him and poured olive oil and wine on his wounds and bandaged them. He put the hurt man on his own donkey and took him to an inn. At the inn, the Samaritan took care of him. ³⁵The next day, the Samaritan brought out two silver coins and gave them to the innkeeper. The Samaritan said, 'Take care of this man. If you spend more money on him, I will pay it back to you when I come again.'"

³⁶Then Jesus said, "Which one of these three men do you think was a neighbor to the man who was attacked by the robbers?"

³⁷The teacher of the law answered, "The one who helped him."

Jesus said to him, "Then go and do the same thing he did!"

> *The priest kept walking. The Levite kept walking. And the Samaritan could have kept walking too. But he didn't. Even though Samaritans and Jews hated each other, he looked past the hatred, saw a man who was hurt, and helped him. It was simply the right thing to do.*
>
> *It's easy to be kind to people who are like you—who look like you and dress like you—but what about people who are different? What about the kid whose clothes are kind of old and worn out? Or whose skin color is darker or lighter? Or who talks different because he came from another country? They may be different, but they are your neighbors too. God made all people "in an amazing and wonderful way" (Psalm 139:14).*

A REAL HERO IS
KIND TO EVERYONE.

HERODIAS WAITS FOR HER CHANCE TO GET RID OF JOHN THE BAPTIST.

HERODIAS WANTS REVENGE

John the Baptist was a messenger from God. He told the people to stop sinning and return to God. But when he told Herodias that she had sinned when she married Herod, Herodias wanted revenge. Did she get it?

from MARK 6:17-29

Herod himself had ordered his soldiers to arrest John, and John was put in prison. Herod did this to please his wife, Herodias. Herodias was the wife of Philip, Herod's brother. But then Herod married her. [18]John told

Herod that it was not lawful for him to be married to his brother's wife. [19]So Herodias hated John and wanted to kill him. But she could not because of Herod. [20]Herod was afraid to kill John because he knew John was a good and holy man. So Herod protected John. Also, Herod enjoyed listening to John preach. But John's preaching always bothered him.

[21]Then the perfect time came for Herodias to cause John's death. It happened on Herod's birthday. Herod gave a dinner party for the most important government leaders, the commanders of his army, and the most important people in Galilee. [22]The daughter of Herodias came to the party and danced. When she danced, Herod and the people eating with him were very pleased.

So King Herod said to the girl, "I will give you anything you want." [23]He promised her, "Anything you ask for I will give to you. I will even give you half of my kingdom."

[24]The girl went to her mother and asked, "What should I ask the king to give me?"

Her mother answered, "Ask for the head of John the Baptist."

[25]Quickly the girl went back to the king. She said to him, "Please give me the head of John the Baptist. Bring it to me now on a platter."

[26]The king was very sad. But he had promised to give the girl anything she wanted. And the people eating there with him had heard his promise. So Herod could not refuse what she asked. [27]Immediately the king sent a soldier to

bring John's head. The soldier went and cut off John's head in the prison ²⁸and brought it back on a platter. He gave it to the girl, and the girl gave it to her mother. ²⁹John's followers heard about what happened. So they came and got John's body and put it in a tomb.

Herodias didn't want to hear that she was doing wrong. So when John the Baptist dared to tell her that she was wrong, she decided to destroy him. She watched and waited for her chance. She watched and waited to do evil.

When thoughts are full of evil, evil is usually what happens. So if you find evil thoughts creeping inside your mind, throw them out! Then, "think about the things that are true and honorable and right and pure and beautiful and respected" (Philippians 4:8). Learn to control your thoughts, so that your thoughts don't control you!

HEROES THINK ABOUT THE THINGS THAT PLEASE GOD.

THE MONEY CHANGERS

People came from all over to worship at the Temple. To do so, they needed to pay the Temple tax with special coins. The money changers were supposed to simply exchange regular money for the Temple coins, but instead they cheated God's people. Would they get caught?

from JOHN 2:12-16

Then Jesus went to the town of Capernaum with his mother, brothers and his followers. They all stayed in Capernaum for a few days. ¹³But it was almost time for the Jewish Passover Feast. So Jesus went to Jerusalem. ¹⁴In the Temple he found men selling cattle, sheep, and doves.

He saw others sitting at tables, exchanging money. [15]Jesus made a whip out of cords. Then he forced all these men, with the sheep and cattle, to leave the Temple. He turned over the tables and scattered the money of the men who were exchanging it. [16]Then he said to those who were selling pigeons, "Take these things out of here! Don't make my Father's house a place for buying and selling!"

The money changers were cheating God's people in the Temple! Jesus was furious, and he chased them out of the Temple. Yes, Jesus was angry, but he used his anger to make things right.

When you see something that is wrong or unfair, it's okay to get angry. It's what you do with that anger that matters. Don't scream. Don't throw a fit. Instead, try to find a way to make it right. Is there someone who is always picked last for the team? When you're the captain, pick him first. Do you see people sleeping on the streets? Have a yard sale with some of your toys and give the money to a shelter. Use the things that make you angry to make it right.

HEROES WORK TO MAKE THINGS RIGHT.

THE WIDOW'S GIFT

There was a poor widow who didn't have much to give. Did her tiny gift even matter?

from MARK 12:41-44

Jesus sat near the Temple money box where people put their gifts. He watched the people put in their money. Many rich people gave large sums of money. ⁴²Then a poor widow came and gave two very small copper coins. These coins were not worth even a penny.

⁴³Jesus called his followers to him. He said, "I tell you the truth. This poor widow gave only two small coins. But she really gave more than all those rich people. ⁴⁴The rich

have plenty; they gave only what they did not need. This woman is very poor. But she gave all she had. And she needed that money to help her live."

The rich would often make a big show out of giving their gifts at the Temple. They wanted everyone to see how much they gave. They cared more about praise from the people than about pleasing God.

The widow did not make a show. Her gift was tiny, but it was all that she had, and she gave it to God. She didn't care if anyone noticed; she only wanted to please God.

Jesus asks you to be careful when you give to God: "Your giving should be done in secret. Your Father can see what is done in secret, and he will reward you" (Matthew 6:4). Heroes know that the best praise comes from God, not men.

HEROES GIVE TO PLEASE GOD, NOT TO BE PRAISED.

The Woman Who Washed Jesus' Feet

It was a simple act of love for her Savior. Some said she was foolish and sinful, but what did Jesus say?

from LUKE 7:21-50

At that time, Jesus healed many people of their sicknesses, diseases, and evil spirits. He healed many blind people so that they could see again. . . .

³⁰But the Pharisees and teachers of the law refused to accept God's plan for themselves.

³⁶One of the Pharisees asked Jesus to eat with him. Jesus went into the Pharisee's house and sat at the table. ³⁷A sinful woman in the town learned that Jesus was eating at the Pharisee's house. So she brought an alabaster jar of perfume. ³⁸She stood at Jesus' feet, crying, and began to wash his feet with her tears. She dried his feet with her hair, kissed them many times and rubbed them with the perfume. ³⁹The Pharisee who asked Jesus to come to his house saw this. He thought to himself, "If Jesus were a prophet, he would know that the woman who is touching him is a sinner!"

⁴⁰Jesus said to the Pharisee, "Simon, I have something to say to you."

Simon said, "Teacher, tell me."

⁴¹Jesus said, "There were two men. Both men owed money to the same banker. One man owed the banker 500 silver coins. The other man owed the banker 50 silver coins. ⁴²The men had no money; so they could not pay what they owed. But the banker told the men that they did not have to pay him. Which one of the two men will love the banker more?"

⁴³Simon, the Pharisee, answered, "I think it would be the one who owed him the most money."

Jesus said to Simon, "You are right." ⁴⁴Then Jesus turned toward the woman and said to Simon, "Do you see this woman? When I came into your house, you gave me no water for my feet. But she washed my feet with her tears and dried my feet with her hair. ⁴⁵You did not kiss me, but she has been kissing my feet since I came in! ⁴⁶You did not rub my head with oil, but she rubbed my feet with perfume. ⁴⁷I tell you that her many sins are forgiven. This is clear because she showed great love. But the person who has only a little to be forgiven will feel only a little love."

⁴⁸Then Jesus said to her, "Your sins are forgiven."

⁴⁹The people sitting at the table began to think to themselves, "Who is this man? How can he forgive sins?"

⁵⁰Jesus said to the woman, "Because you believed, you are saved from your sins. Go in peace."

She didn't try to talk to him or ask him for anything. But she washed Jesus' feet with her tears. She was crying because she knew how many mistakes she had made. The Pharisee said she was sinful, and he believed Jesus shouldn't even let her touch him. But Jesus said she was forgiven and saved. Jesus saw the person whom others refused to notice—and he blessed her.

Jesus came to forgive and to save. He came for all those who know they have done wrong and who now want to make it right. He "came to find lost people and save them" (Luke 19:10). He came for you. Tell him about your sins and your mistakes. Pour out your heart to him. He will forgive you. That's why he came.

REAL HEROES ASK GOD TO FORGIVE THEIR SINS.

NICODEMUS SEARCHES FOR ANSWERS IN THE NIGHT.

Nicodemus Questions Jesus

Nicodemus was a Pharisee and a member of the Jewish ruling council. Most Pharisees wanted to kill Jesus, but Nicodemus wanted to ask him some questions.

from JOHN 3:1-21

There was a man named Nicodemus who was one of the Pharisees. He was an important Jewish leader. [2]One night Nicodemus came to Jesus. He said, "Teacher, we know that you are a teacher sent from God. No one can do the miracles you do, unless God is with him."

[3]Jesus answered, "I tell you the truth. Unless one is born again, he cannot be in God's kingdom."

[4]Nicodemus said, "But if a man is already old, how can he be born again? He cannot enter his mother's body again. So how can he be born a second time?"

[5]But Jesus answered, "I tell you the truth. Unless one is born from water and the Spirit, he cannot enter God's kingdom. [6]A person's body is born from his human parents. But a person's spiritual life is born from the Spirit. [7]Don't be surprised when I tell you, 'You must all be born again.' [8]The wind blows where it wants to go. You hear the wind blow. But you don't know where the wind comes from or where it is going. It is the same with every person who is born from the Spirit."

[9]Nicodemus asked, "How can all this be possible?"

[10]Jesus said, "You are an important teacher in Israel. But you still don't understand these things? [11]I tell you the truth. We talk about what we know. We tell about what we have seen. But you don't accept what we tell you. [12]I have told you about things here on earth, but you do not believe me. So surely you will not believe me if I tell you about the things of heaven! [13]The only one who has ever gone up to heaven is the One who came down from heaven—the Son of Man.

[14]"Moses lifted up the snake in the desert. It is the same with the Son of Man. The Son of Man must be lifted up too. [15]Then everyone who believes in him can have eternal life.

16"For God loved the world so much that he gave his only Son. God gave his Son so that whoever believes in him may not be lost, but have eternal life. 17God did not send his Son into the world to judge the world guilty, but to save the world through him. 18He who believes in God's Son is not judged guilty. He who does not believe has already been judged guilty, because he has not believed in God's only Son. 19People are judged by this fact: I am the Light from God that has come into the world. But men did not want light. . . . 21He who follows the true way comes to the light. Then the light will show that the things he has done were done through God."

Nicodemus had seen and heard about the many miracles that Jesus had done. He knew how much the other Pharisees hated Jesus, but he had some questions. So he went to Jesus, and Jesus had all the answers.

As you grow up, you will hear a lot of things about God and Jesus, and about how to live your life. Some things are good and true, but others are not. How do you know which is which? Do just like Nicodemus did—go to Jesus and ask him. For "all Scripture is given by God and is useful for teaching . . . how to live right" (2 Timothy 3:16).

REAL HEROES KNOW THAT JESUS
STILL HAS ALL THE ANSWERS.

THE PHARISEES PLAN TO KILL JESUS

The Pharisees were the rulers of the Jewish Temple. They were supposed to be God's holy people. But they loved power more than they loved God. So when Jesus began to teach a new way, they didn't like it.

from MATTHEW 9:9-12:14; 21:45-23:12

The Pharisees didn't like that Jesus came to teach all people . . .

Matthew was sitting in the tax office. Jesus said to him, "Follow me." And Matthew stood up and followed Jesus.

¹⁰Jesus had dinner at Matthew's house. Many tax collectors and "sinners" came and ate with Jesus and his followers. ¹¹The Pharisees saw this and asked Jesus' followers, "Why does your teacher eat with tax collectors and 'sinners'?"

¹²Jesus heard the Pharisees ask this. So he said, "Healthy people don't need a doctor. Only the sick need a doctor. ¹³Go and learn what this means: 'I want faithful love more than I want animal sacrifices.' I did not come to invite good people. I came to invite sinners."

The Pharisees cared more about rules than people . . .

12 ¹⁰In the synagogue, there was a man with a crippled hand. Some Jews there were looking for a reason to accuse Jesus of doing wrong. So they asked him, "Is it right to heal on the Sabbath day?"

¹¹Jesus answered, "If any of you has a sheep, and it falls into a ditch on the Sabbath day, then you will take the sheep and help it out of the ditch. ¹²Surely a man is more important than a sheep. So the law of Moses allows people to do good things on the Sabbath day."

¹³Then Jesus said to the man with the crippled hand,

"Let me see your hand." The man put his hand out, and the hand became well again, the same as the other hand. [14]But the Pharisees left and made plans to kill Jesus.

The Pharisees were afraid . . .

21 [45]The leading priests and the Pharisees heard these stories that Jesus told. They knew he was talking about them. [46]They wanted to arrest him. But they were afraid of the people, because the people believed that Jesus was a prophet.

Jesus warned his followers . . .

23 [2]"The teachers of the law and the Pharisees have the authority to tell you what the law of Moses says. [3]So you should obey and follow whatever they tell you. But their lives are not good examples for you to follow. They tell you to do things, but they don't do the things themselves. [4]They make strict rules and try to force people to obey them. But they themselves will not try to follow any of those rules.

5"The reason they do good things is so other people will see them. They make the boxes of Scriptures that they wear bigger and bigger. And they make their special prayer clothes very long so that people will notice them. 6Those Pharisees and teachers of the law love to have the most important seats at the feasts. And they love to have the most important seats in the synagogues. 7They love people to show respect to them in the marketplaces. . . . 11He who serves you as a servant is the greatest among you. 12Whoever makes himself great will be made humble. Whoever makes himself humble will be made great."

The Pharisees were supposed to love God's people, but instead they loved power and money. They were supposed to lead God's people to him, but instead they led them away from his Son. They were supposed to worship Christ, but instead they killed him. The Pharisees let power and money keep them from God.

Is there anything keeping you from God? If there is, put it away from you. Friends are wonderful, but if they keep you away from God—find new friends. Ballgames are exciting, but if they keep you away from worship—find another time to watch and play. Choose to put God first, and nothing can separate you from his love.

HEROES CHOOSE TO PUT GOD FIRST.

JUDAS PLANS TO BETRAY JESUS.

JUDAS, THE BETRAYER

Judas was one of those closest to Jesus. But his love of money led him to betray the only One who could save him.

from MATTHEW 26:14–27:5

Then 1 of the 12 followers went to talk to the leading priests. This was the follower named Judas Iscariot. [15]He said, "I will give Jesus to you. What will you pay me for doing this?" The priests gave Judas 30 silver coins. [16]After that, Judas waited for the best time to give Jesus to the priests.

[17]On the first day of the feast of Unleavened Bread,

the followers came to Jesus. They said, "We will prepare everything for you to eat the Passover Feast. Where do you want to have the feast?"

¹⁸Jesus answered, "Go into the city to a certain man. Tell him that the Teacher says, 'The chosen time is near. I will have the Passover Feast with my followers at your house.'" ¹⁹The followers did what Jesus told them to do, and they prepared the Passover Feast.

²⁰In the evening Jesus was sitting at the table with his 12 followers. ²¹They were all eating. Then Jesus said, "I tell you the truth. One of you 12 will turn against me."

²²This made the followers very sad. Each one said to Jesus, "Surely, Lord, I am not the one who will turn against you. Am I?"

²³Jesus answered, "The man who has dipped his hand with me into the bowl is the one who will turn against me. ²⁴The Son of Man will die. The Scriptures say this will happen. But how terrible it will be for the person who gives the Son of Man to be killed. It would be better for him if he had never been born."

²⁵Then Judas said to Jesus, "Teacher, surely I am not the one. Am I?" (Judas is the one who would give Jesus to his enemies.)

Jesus answered, "Yes, it is you."

²⁶While they were eating, Jesus took some bread. He thanked God for it and broke it. Then he gave it to his followers and said, "Take this bread and eat it. This bread is my body."

²⁷Then Jesus took a cup. He thanked God for it and gave it to the followers. He said, "Every one of you drink this. ²⁸This is my blood which begins the new agreement that God makes with his people. This blood is poured out for many to forgive their sins. ²⁹I tell you this: I will not drink of this fruit of the vine again until that day when I drink it new with you in my Father's kingdom." . . .

³⁶Then Jesus went with his followers to a place called Gethsemane. He said to them, "Sit here while I go over there and pray." ³⁷He told Peter and the two sons of Zebedee to come with him. Then Jesus began to be very sad and troubled. ³⁸He said to Peter and the two sons of Zebedee, "My heart is full of sorrow and breaking with sadness. Stay here with me and watch."

³⁹Then Jesus walked a little farther away from them. He fell to the ground and prayed, "My Father, if it is possible, do not give me this cup of suffering. But do what you want, not what I want." ⁴⁰Then Jesus went back to his followers and found them asleep. Jesus said to Peter, "You men could not stay awake with me for one hour? ⁴¹Stay awake and pray for strength against temptation. Your spirit wants to do what is right. But your body is weak."

⁴²Then Jesus went away a second time. He prayed, "My Father, if it is not possible for this painful thing to be taken

from me, and if I must do it, then I pray that what you want will be done."

[43]Then Jesus went back to the followers. Again he found them asleep, because their eyes were heavy. [44]So Jesus left them and went away one more time and prayed. This third time he prayed, he said the same thing.

[45]Then Jesus went back to the followers and said, "You are still sleeping and resting? The time has come for the Son of Man to be given to sinful people. [46]Get up. We must go. Here comes the man who has turned against me."

[47]While Jesus was still speaking, Judas came up. Judas was 1 of the 12 followers. He had many people with him. They had been sent from the leading priests and the older leaders of the people. They carried swords and clubs. [48]Judas had planned to give them a signal. He had said, "The man I kiss is Jesus. Arrest him." [49]At once Judas went to Jesus and said, "Greetings, Teacher!" Then Judas kissed him.

[50]Jesus answered, "Friend, do the thing you came to do."

Then the men came and grabbed Jesus and arrested him. . . . [55]Then Jesus said to the crowd, "You came to get me with swords and clubs as if I were a criminal. Every day I sat in the Temple teaching. You did not arrest me there. [56]But all these things have happened so that it will be as the prophets wrote." Then all of Jesus' followers left him and ran away. . . .

27 [3]Judas saw that they had decided to kill Jesus. . . He was very sorry for what he had done. So he took the 30 silver coins back to the priests and the leaders.

[4]Judas said, "I sinned. I gave you an innocent man to be killed."

The leaders answered, "What is that to us? That's your problem, not ours."

[5]So Judas threw the money into the Temple. Then he went off and hanged himself.

> *Judas was willing to betray Jesus, to turn him over to the Pharisees who wanted to kill him—all for a few silver coins. The money was more important to Judas than his friendship with Jesus. First Timothy 6:10 says that "the love of money causes all kinds of evil."*
>
> *It's okay to have money and to work to get more money. The trouble comes when money becomes more important than God, your family, and your friends. Money can be stolen and treasure can be destroyed, but the love of God and others builds up heavenly treasures that will be yours forever.*

A HERO'S TREASURE CHEST ISN'T FILLED WITH GOLD; IT'S FILLED WITH LOVE.

PETER SAYS HE DOES NOT KNOW JESUS.

PETER: A HERO MAKES A MISTAKE

Peter was a true friend to Jesus and one of his closest disciples. But even true friends make mistakes.

from LUKE 22:33-62

Before Jesus was arrested, each of his disciples said that they would never desert him . . .

Peter said to Jesus, "Lord, I am ready to go to prison with you. I will even die with you!"

³⁴But Jesus said, "Peter, before the rooster crows tonight, you will say you don't know me. You will say this three times!"

Later, after Judas had betrayed Jesus . . .

⁵⁴They arrested Jesus and took him away. They brought him into the house of the high priest. Peter followed them, but he did not go near Jesus. ⁵⁵The soldiers started a fire in the middle of the courtyard and sat together. Peter sat with them. ⁵⁶A servant girl saw Peter sitting there near the light. She looked closely at Peter's face and said, "This man was also with him!"

⁵⁷But Peter said this was not true. He said, "Girl, I don't know him."

⁵⁸A short time later, another person saw Peter and said, "You are also one of them."

But Peter said, "Man, I am not!"

⁵⁹About an hour later, another man insisted, "It is true! This man was with him. He is from Galilee!"

⁶⁰But Peter said, "Man, I don't know what you are talking about!"

Immediately, while Peter was still speaking, a rooster crowed. ⁶¹Then the Lord turned and looked straight at Peter. And Peter remembered what the Lord had said: "Before the rooster crows tonight, you will say three times that you don't know me." [62]Then Peter went outside and cried with much pain in his heart.

Peter was a great hero of the faith. But he had just seen armed guards and soldiers arrest Jesus. This was a dangerous situation, and Peter was frightened. So when the people accused him of being Jesus' follower, he lied.

Fear can lead you into doing things that you know are wrong. Fear of getting into trouble can lead you to lie. Fear of being teased can lead you to tease someone else. Fear can lead you to sin. Peter's mistake wasn't being afraid; it was letting fear cause him to sin.

Don't let fear be your leader. Make Jesus your leader, for he said, "In this world you will have trouble. But be brave! I have defeated the world" (John 16:33).

HEROES LET JESUS LEAD THE WAY!

PILATE WASHES HIS HANDS AFTER ORDERING THE CRUCIFIXION OF JESUS.

PILATE WASHES HIS HANDS

The Jewish leaders wanted Jesus killed, but only the Roman rulers could execute someone. So they took Jesus to Pilate, the Roman governor. But why did Pilate wash his hands? And why was that so terrible?

from MATTHEW 27:11-26

Jesus stood before Pilate the governor. Pilate asked him, "Are you the King of the Jews?"

Jesus answered, "Yes, I am."

[12]When the leading priests and the older leaders accused Jesus, he said nothing.

¹³So Pilate said to Jesus, "Don't you hear these people accusing you of all these things?"

¹⁴But Jesus said nothing in answer to Pilate. Pilate was very surprised at this.

¹⁵Every year at the time of Passover the governor would free one person from prison. This was always a person the people wanted to be set free. ¹⁶At that time there was a man in prison who was known to be very bad. His name was Barabbas. ¹⁷All the people gathered at Pilate's house. Pilate said, "Which man do you want me to free: Barabbas, or Jesus who is called the Christ?" ¹⁸Pilate knew that the people gave Jesus to him because they were jealous.

¹⁹Pilate said these things while he was sitting on the judge's seat. While he was sitting there, his wife sent a message to him. The message said, "Don't do anything to that man. He is not guilty. Today I had a dream about him, and it troubled me very much."

²⁰But the leading priests and older leaders told the crowd to ask for Barabbas to be freed and for Jesus to be killed.

²¹Pilate said, "I have Barabbas and Jesus. Which do you want me to set free for you?"

The people answered, "Barabbas!"

²²Pilate asked, "What should I do with Jesus, the one called the Christ?"

They all answered, "Kill him on a cross!"

²³Pilate asked, "Why do you want me to kill him? What wrong has he done?"

But they shouted louder, "Kill him on a cross!"

²⁴Pilate saw that he could do nothing about this, and a riot was starting. So he took some water and washed his hands in front of the crowd. Then he said, "I am not guilty of this man's death. . . ."

²⁶Then Pilate freed Barabbas. Pilate told some of the soldiers to beat Jesus with whips. Then he gave Jesus to the soldiers to be killed on a cross.

Pilate knew that Jesus was innocent, but he was afraid that the Jewish leaders would cause trouble for him. So Pilate ordered that Jesus be killed. Then he washed his hands to say that he was not responsible.

If you know something wrong is about to happen, can you really just wash your hands and walk away? God hopes that you won't. God hopes that you will be brave enough to say what is right. If a song uses God's name in a bad way, turn it off. If someone tells you that God isn't real, invite that person to church with you to hear for himself. God's Word says, "Do not be afraid! Continue talking to people and don't be quiet! I am with you" (Acts 18:9–10). God never leaves a hero alone.

HEROES KNOW THAT GOD WILL NEVER LEAVE THEM.

JESUS DIES ON THE CROSS.

THE SOLDIERS AT THE CROSS

Jesus, the Son of God, had been sentenced to die on a cross. It couldn't possibly get any worse for Jesus . . . or could it?

from MATTHEW 27:27-54

Pilate's soldiers took Jesus into the governor's palace. All the soldiers gathered around Jesus. [28]They took off his clothes and put a red robe on him. [29]Then the soldiers used thorny branches to make a crown. They put this crown of thorns on Jesus' head. They put a stick in his right hand. Then the soldiers bowed before Jesus and made fun of him. They said, "Hail, King of the Jews!" ³⁰They spit on Jesus. Then they took his stick and hit him on the head many times. ³¹After they finished making fun of Jesus, the soldiers took off the robe and put his own clothes on him again. Then they led Jesus away to be killed on a cross.

³²The soldiers were going out of the city with Jesus. They forced another man to carry the cross to be used for Jesus. This man was Simon, from Cyrene. ³³They all came to the place called Golgotha. (Golgotha means the Place of the Skull.) ³⁴At Golgotha, the soldiers gave Jesus wine to drink. This wine was mixed with gall. He tasted the wine but refused to drink it. ³⁵The soldiers nailed Jesus to a cross. They threw lots to decide who would get his clothes. ³⁶The soldiers sat there and continued watching him. ³⁷They put a sign above Jesus' head with the charge against him written on it. The sign read: "THIS IS JESUS, THE KING OF THE JEWS." ³⁸Two robbers were nailed to crosses beside Jesus, one on the right and the other on the left. ³⁹People walked by and insulted Jesus. They shook their heads, ⁴⁰saying, "You said you could destroy the Temple and build it again in three days. So save yourself! Come down from that cross, if you are really the Son of God!"

⁴¹The leading priests, the teachers of the law, and the older Jewish leaders were also there. These men made fun of Jesus ⁴²and said, "He saved other people, but he can't save himself! People say he is the King of Israel! If he is the

King, then let him come down now from the cross. Then we will believe in him. [43]He trusts in God. So let God save him now, if God really wants him. He himself said, 'I am the Son of God.'" [44]And in the same way, the robbers who were being killed on crosses beside Jesus also insulted him.

[45]At noon the whole country became dark. This darkness lasted for three hours. [46]About three o'clock Jesus cried out in a loud voice, "Eli, Eli, lama sabachthani?" This means, "My God, my God, why have you left me alone?"

[47]Some of the people standing there heard this. They said, "He is calling Elijah."

[48]Quickly one of them ran and got a sponge. He filled the sponge with vinegar and tied it to a stick. Then he used the stick to give the sponge to Jesus to drink from it. [49]But the others said, "Don't bother him. We want to see if Elijah will come to save him."

[50]Again Jesus cried out in a loud voice. Then he died. [51]Then the curtain in the Temple split into two pieces. The tear started at the top and tore all the way down to the bottom. Also, the earth shook and rocks broke apart. [52]The graves opened, and many of God's people who had died were raised from death. [53]They came out of the graves after Jesus was raised from death. They went into the holy city, and many people saw them.

[54]The army officer and the soldiers guarding Jesus saw this earthquake and everything else that happened. They were very frightened and said, "He really was the Son of God!"

Death on a Roman cross was terrible, but the soldiers made it even more terrible. They made fun of Jesus. They hit him. They even spat on the Son of God. And then they led him away to die on a cross. They were mean and cruel, just because they could be.

It's a choice that you have to make every day. Do you choose love and gentleness, or do you choose meanness and cruelty? This is what God asks of you: "Show mercy to others; be kind, humble, gentle, and patient. . . . but most important, love each other" (Colossians 3:12, 14). That's what heroes do.

REAL HEROES ARE BRAVE ENOUGH TO LOVE OTHERS.

Joseph of Arimathea

Jewish law said that Jesus' body had to be removed from the cross before the Sabbath began. But with all the Jewish leaders watching, was anyone brave enough to claim it?

from JOHN 19:38-42; LUKE 23:48-56

Later, a man named Joseph from Arimathea asked Pilate if he could take the body of Jesus. (Joseph was a secret follower of Jesus, because he was afraid of the Jews.) Pilate gave his permission. So Joseph came and took Jesus' body away. [39]Nicodemus went with Joseph. Nicodemus was the man who earlier had come to Jesus at night. He brought about 75 pounds of spices. This was a mixture of myrrh and aloes. [40]These two men took Jesus' body and wrapped it with the spices in pieces of linen cloth. (This is how the Jews bury people.) [41]In the place where Jesus was killed, there was a garden. In the garden was a new tomb where no one had ever been buried. [42]The men laid Jesus in that tomb because it was near, and the Jews were preparing to start their Sabbath day.

Luke 23

[48]Many people had gathered there to watch this thing. When they saw what happened, they returned home. They beat their chests because they were so sad. [49]Those who were close friends of Jesus were there. Some were women who had followed Jesus from Galilee. They all stood far away from the cross and watched. . . .

[55]The women who had come from Galilee with Jesus followed Joseph. They saw the tomb and saw inside where

the body of Jesus was laid. [56]Then the women left to prepare perfumes and spices.

On the Sabbath day they rested, as the law of Moses commanded.

It was a dangerous time to be a follower of Jesus. Jesus himself had just been killed—what would be done to his followers? But two men were brave enough to go to Pilate, to take Jesus' body, and to lay him in a tomb. They were brave enough to step up and say, "We follow Jesus."

It isn't always easy to say that you believe in Jesus. When you are the only one in your class who believes. When others are making fun of God. When believing in God means you can't do what your friends are doing. But Jesus promises that "if anyone stands before other people and says he believes in me, then I will say that he belongs to me. I will say this before my Father in heaven" (Matthew 10:32).

REAL HEROES ARE BRAVE ENOUGH TO SAY THEY BELIEVE IN JESUS.

THE WOMEN
FIND AN EMPTY
TOMB.

THE WOMEN AT THE TOMB

They stayed with Jesus at the cross. They followed as Joseph and Nicodemus laid his body in the tomb. When the Sabbath was over, they returned to the tomb to take care of Jesus' body. But what did they find there?

from LUKE 24:1-12

Very early on the first day of the week, the women came to the tomb where Jesus' body was laid. They brought the spices they had prepared. ²They found that the stone had been rolled away from the entrance of the tomb. ³They went in, but they did not find the body of the Lord Jesus. ⁴While they were wondering about this, two men in shining clothes suddenly stood beside them. ⁵The women were very afraid; they bowed their heads to the ground. The men said to the women, "Why are you looking for a living person here? This is a place for the dead. ⁶Jesus is not here. He has risen from death! Do you remember what he said in Galilee? ⁷He said that the Son of Man must be given to evil men, be killed on a cross, and rise from death on the third day." ⁸Then the women remembered what Jesus had said.

⁹The women left the tomb and told all these things to the 11 apostles and the other followers. ¹⁰These women were Mary Magdalene, Joanna, Mary the mother of James, and some other women. The women told the apostles everything that had happened at the tomb. ¹¹But they did not believe the women. It sounded like nonsense. ¹²But Peter got up and ran to the tomb. He looked in, but he saw only the cloth that Jesus' body had been wrapped in. Peter went away to be alone, wondering about what had happened.

It wasn't fun at the cross, or following Jesus' body to the tomb. The women weren't looking forward to going inside the tomb. Although they weren't forced to do these things and no one praised them for it, these were things that needed to be done. And God in heaven saw them and loved them for doing them.

Some things you do for God are fun—like singing praises and being with friends at church. Other things are not so much fun—like nursing someone who is sick or picking up the trash after the church party is over. You might not be forced to do these things, and your work might not be noticed. But if you choose to do these things, God in heaven will see you and love you for it.

HEROES DO WHAT NEEDS TO BE DONE WITHOUT COMPLAINING.

JESUS
RETURNS TO
THE FATHER.

Jesus Returns to Heaven

After Jesus rose from the grave, he stayed with his apostles 40 days. He promised to send them the Holy Spirit, who would help them understand and remember his teachings. Then he gathered his closest disciples to him for one more miracle.

from MATTHEW 28:16-20; ACTS 1:8-11

The 11 followers went to Galilee. They went to the mountain where Jesus told them to go. ¹⁷On the mountain they saw Jesus and worshiped him. But some of them did not believe that it was really Jesus.

¹⁸Then Jesus came to them and said, "All power in heaven and on earth is given to me. ¹⁹So go and make followers of all people in the world. Baptize them in the name of the Father and the Son and the Holy Spirit. ²⁰Teach them to obey everything that I have told you. You can be sure that I will be with you always. I will continue with you until the end of the world."

Acts 1

Jesus said . . .

1 ⁸The Holy Spirit will come to you. Then you will receive power. You will be my witnesses—in Jerusalem, in all of Judea, in Samaria, and in every part of the world."

⁹After he said this, as they were watching, he was lifted up. A cloud hid him from their sight. ¹⁰As he was going, they were looking into the sky. Suddenly, two men wearing white clothes stood beside them. ¹¹They said, "Men of Galilee, why are standing here looking into the sky? You saw Jesus taken away from you into heaven. He will come back in the same way you saw him go."

Jesus was the Son of God. He left the wonder and power of heaven and came to earth as a helpless infant, born in a dusty stable in a tiny town. He was a child who grew up, just as you are growing up. Then, when he was grown, he went out to teach the people how to be saved. For that, he was beaten and killed on a cross. Why would Jesus do that?

Jesus himself tells you why: "For God loved the world so much that he gave his only Son. God gave his Son so that whoever believes in him may not be lost, but have eternal life" (John 3:16).

You can do great things for God, wonderfully heroic things. But you can never work your way to heaven. Jesus is the only way. Believe in him and obey him and love him with all your heart. Heroes do their best to follow the Greatest Hero in everything that they do.

HEROES KNOW THAT JESUS IS
THE ONLY WAY TO GOD.

STEPHEN IS
STONED.

STEPHEN FORGIVES

Stephen was preaching and teaching the Good News about Jesus, but not everyone wanted that news to be told. How far did they go to stop him?

from ACTS 6:8-7:60

Stephen was richly blessed by God. God gave him the power to do great miracles and signs among the people. ⁹But some Jews were against him. They belonged to a synagogue of Free Men (as it was called). (This synagogue was also for Jews from Cyrene and from Alexandria.) Jews from Cilicia and Asia were also with them. They all came and argued with Stephen.

¹⁰But the Spirit was helping him to speak with wisdom. His words were so strong that they could not argue with him. ¹¹So they paid some men to say, "We heard him say things against Moses and against God!"

¹²This upset the people, the older Jewish leaders, and the teachers of the law. They came to Stephen, grabbed him and brought him to a meeting of the Jewish leaders. ¹³They brought in some men to tell lies about Stephen. They said, "This man is always saying things against this holy place and the law of Moses. ¹⁴We heard him say that Jesus from Nazareth will destroy this place. He also said that Jesus will change the things that Moses told us to do." ¹⁵All the people in the meeting were watching Stephen closely. His face looked like the face of an angel.

7 ¹The high priest said to Stephen, "Are these things true?"

Then Stephen answered by reminding them of the stories of Abraham, Joseph, Moses, and Joshua.

⁴⁴"The Holy Tent where God spoke to our fathers was with the Jews in the desert. God told Moses how to

make this Tent. He made it like the plan God showed him. [45]Later, Joshua led our fathers to capture the lands of the other nations. Our people went in, and God drove the other people out. When our people went into this new land, they took with them this same Tent. They received this Tent from their fathers and kept it until the time of David. [46]God was very pleased with David. He asked God to let him build a house for him, the God of Jacob. [47]But Solomon was the one who built the Temple.

[48]"But the Most High does not live in houses that men build with their hands. This is what the prophet says:

> [49]'Heaven is my throne.
>   The earth is my footstool.
> So do you think you can build a house for me?
>   says the Lord.
>   There is no place where I need to rest.
> [50]Remember, I made all these things!'"
>   Isaiah 66:1–2

[51]Stephen continued speaking, "You stubborn Jewish leaders! You have not given your hearts to God! You won't listen to him! You are always against what the Holy Spirit is trying to tell you. Your ancestors were like this, and

you are just like them! [52]Your fathers tried to hurt every prophet who ever lived. Those prophets said long ago that the Righteous One would come. But your fathers killed them. And now you have turned against the Righteous One and killed him. [53]You received the law of Moses, which God gave you through his angels. But you don't obey it!"

[54]When the leaders heard Stephen saying all these things, they became very angry. They were so mad that they were grinding their teeth at Stephen. [55]But Stephen was full of the Holy Spirit. He looked up to heaven and saw the glory of God. He saw Jesus standing at God's right side. [56]He said, "Look! I see heaven open. And I see the Son of Man standing at God's right side!"

[57]Then they all shouted loudly. They covered their ears with their hands and all ran at Stephen. [58]They took him out of the city and threw stones at him until he was dead. The men who told lies against Stephen left their coats with a young man named Saul. [59]While they were throwing stones, Stephen prayed, "Lord Jesus, receive my spirit!" [60]He fell on his knees and cried in a loud voice, "Lord, do not hold this sin against them!" After Stephen said this, he died.

The Jewish leaders didn't want the people to hear about Jesus, so they argued with Stephen. When that didn't stop him, they paid men to tell lies about him. And when Stephen still wouldn't back down, they stoned him to death. But what were Stephen's last words? Were they about revenge, or anger, or hatred? No. He asked God to forgive them of this sin.

It happens. Someone, somewhere, someday will be mean to you. And that will be your chance to show that person what a real hero looks like. When someone calls you names, pushes in front of you in the line, or hurts your feelings, don't "do wrong to a person to pay him back for doing wrong to you. Or do not insult someone to pay him back for insulting you. But ask God to bless that person" (1 Peter 3:9). It's what heroes do.

HEROES FORGIVE
BECAUSE THEY KNOW THAT
THEY ARE FORGIVEN.

PHILIP
BAPTIZES THE
ETHIOPIAN.

PHILIP PLANTS A SEED

After Jesus returned to heaven, his apostles taught everyone who would listen. Philip was preaching in Samaria when an angel sent him on a special mission.

from ACTS 8:26-39

An angel of the Lord spoke to Philip. The angel said, "Get ready and go south. Go to the road that leads down to Gaza from Jerusalem—the desert road." 27So Philip got ready and went. On the road he saw a man from Ethiopia, a eunuch. He was an important officer in the service of Candace, the queen of the Ethiopians. He was responsible for taking care of all her money. He had gone to Jerusalem to worship, and ²⁸now he was on his way home. He was sitting in his chariot and reading from the book of Isaiah, the prophet. ²⁹The Spirit said to Philip, "Go to that chariot and stay near it."

³⁰So Philip ran toward the chariot. He heard the man reading from Isaiah, the prophet. Philip asked, "Do you understand what you are reading?"

³¹He answered, "How can I understand? I need someone to explain it to me!" Then he invited Philip to . . . sit with him. ³²The verse of Scripture that he was reading was this:

> "He was like a sheep being led to be killed.
>   He was quiet, as a sheep is quiet while its
>   wool is being cut.
> He said nothing.
>   ³³He was shamed and was treated unfairly.
> He died without children to continue his family.
>   His life on earth has ended."
>   Isaiah 53:7–8

³⁴The officer said to Philip, "Please tell me, who is the prophet talking about? Is he talking about himself or about someone else?" ³⁵Philip . . . started with this same Scripture and told the man the Good News about Jesus.

³⁶While they were traveling down the road, they came to

some water. The officer said, "Look! Here is water! What is stopping me from being baptized?" [37][Philip answered, "If you believe with all your heart, you can." The officer said, "I believe that Jesus Christ is the Son of God."] [38]Then the officer commanded the chariot to stop. Both Philip and the officer went down into the water, and Philip baptized him. [39]When they came up out of the water, the Spirit of the Lord took Philip away; the officer never saw him again. The officer continued on his way home, full of joy.

Big things, like towering trees, start with little things, like tiny seeds. And in the kingdom of God, everything starts with obeying God. Philip obeyed and went to the desert road. There he told one man about Jesus. That one man then took the Good News about Jesus to a whole new country! All because Philip was willing to take a little walk and plant a little seed.

Are you willing to plant a little seed? Will you tell a friend that Jesus loves her? Give up your Saturday to wash cars to help a missionary? Or share your allowance with God? It may seem like a small thing, like a tiny seed. But heroes know God can turn tiny seeds into towering trees for his kingdom.

HEROES PLANT SEEDS OF FAITH FOR GOD WHEREVER THEY GO!

JESUS SPEAKS
TO SAUL ON
THE ROAD TO
DAMASCUS.

Saul: A Hero in the Making

Saul was determined to wipe out the Christians in Jerusalem. He had them beaten and thrown in jail. He even held the cloaks of those who stoned Stephen. So when he headed for Damascus, it could only mean trouble . . . or could it?

from ACTS 9:1-22

In Jerusalem Saul was still trying to frighten the followers of the Lord by saying he would kill them. So he went to the high priest [2]and asked him to write letters to the synagogues in the city of Damascus. Saul wanted the high priest to give him the authority to find people in Damascus who were followers of Christ's Way. If he found any there, men or women, he would arrest them and bring them back to Jerusalem.

[3]So Saul went to Damascus. As he came near the city, a bright light from heaven suddenly flashed around him. [4]Saul fell to the ground. He heard a voice saying to him, "Saul, Saul! Why are you doing things against me?"

[5]Saul said, "Who are you, Lord?"

The voice answered, "I am Jesus. I am the One you are trying to hurt. [6]Get up now and go into the city. Someone there will tell you what you must do."

[7]The men traveling with Saul stood there, but they said nothing. They heard the voice, but they saw no one. [8]Saul got up from the ground. He opened his eyes, but he could not see. So the men with Saul took his hand and led him into Damascus. [9]For three days Saul could not see, and he did not eat or drink.

[10]There was a follower of Jesus in Damascus named Ananias. The Lord spoke to Ananias in a vision, "Ananias!"

Ananias answered, "Here I am, Lord."

[11]The Lord said to him, "Get up and go to the street called Straight Street. Find the house of Judas. Ask for a man named Saul from the city of Tarsus. He is there now, praying. [12]Saul has seen a vision. In it a man named Ananias comes to him and lays his hands on him. Then he sees again."

[13]But Ananias answered, "Lord, many people have told me about this man and the terrible things he did to your people in Jerusalem. [14]Now he has come here to Damascus. The leading priests have given him the power to arrest everyone who worships you."

[15]But the Lord said to Ananias, "Go! I have chosen Saul for an important work. He must tell about me to non-Jews, to kings, and to the people of Israel. [16]I will show him how much he must suffer for my name."

[17]So Ananias went to the house of Judas. He laid his hands on Saul and said, "Brother Saul, the Lord Jesus sent me. He is the one you saw on the road on your way here. He sent me so that you can see again and be filled with the Holy Spirit." [18]Immediately, something that looked like fish scales fell from Saul's eyes. He was able to see again! Then Saul got up and was baptized. [19]After eating some food, his strength returned.

Saul stayed with the followers of Jesus in Damascus for a few days. [20]Soon he began to preach about Jesus in the synagogues, saying, "Jesus is the Son of God!"

[21]All the people who heard him were amazed. They said, "This is the man who was in Jerusalem. He was trying to destroy those who trust in this name! He came here to arrest the followers of Jesus and take them back to the leading priests."

[22]But Saul became more and more powerful. His proofs that Jesus is the Christ were so strong that the Jews in Damascus could not argue with him.

Saul was going down the road to Damascus, but in his spirit, he was going down the wrong road altogether. He was threatening and hurting God's people. But Jesus reached out to him and put him on the right road—the road to heaven. Saul—who became Paul— got a do-over.

On the playground, you get do-overs. Ball rolls crooked? Do-over! Stumble and miss the shot? Do-over! Do-overs are wonderful! But do-overs aren't just for the playground. God is all about do-overs. Slip up and tell a fib? Do-over! Get angry and do something you shouldn't? Do-over! When you know you've messed up, ask God for a do-over. God promises that "if we confess our sins, he will forgive our sins" (1 John 1:9)—it's like a do-over!

HEROES AREN'T AFRAID TO ASK FOR A DO-OVER.

Note to Heroes

Life is all about choices. And every day there are new choices to make. Will you choose to be kind or to be mean? Will you choose to love or hate? Will you choose to forgive or will you hold a grudge?

It really all comes down to this: will you choose to live for God or to live for the devil? It truly is your choice. What you decide will make all the difference in your life.

Will you be a hero for God? Will you choose him just as Joshua did when he said, "As for me and my family, we will serve the Lord" (Joshua 24:15)?

REAL HEROES CHOOSE GOD!